POETRY AND THE PHYSICAL VOICE

Also by Francis Berry

Poetry
THE GALLOPING CENTAUR
MORANT BAY AND OTHER POEMS

Criticism
POETS' GRAMMAR
HERBERT READ

Poetry and the Physical Voice

by

FRANCIS BERRY

Routledge and Kegan Paul

LONDON

First published 1962
by Routledge & Kegan Paul Ltd.
Broadway House, 68–74 Carter Lane
*London, E.C.*4

Second impression 1963

Printed in Great Britain
by Richard Clay and Company, Ltd.
Bungay, Suffolk

To
NANCY

Contents

Preface

A VERY brief outline of the argument of *Poetry and the Physical Voice* first appeared in *Books*. Since then expansions were given successively in the form of a BBC Third Programme talk, as papers read at Durham and at the first International Conference on Poetics held in Warsaw and as an essay that appeared in *The Wind and the Rain Yearbook*.

What follows may be regarded as in some ways complementary to the proposition demonstrated in *Poets' Grammar* (1958). If a poem's significance depends much on the pronouns it uses or assumes, on who addresses whom within its boundaries, and on the forms of the verbs employed in its construction, by which we understand whether the events of the poem happened in the past or are to take place in the future or—if the verbs are subjunctive—belong to the order of wishes and regret and so lie outside of time altogether, then the poem's significance also depends on the kind of voice conveying the information. At the simplest level, language which intends one meaning in writing can intend another when spoken. It is not quite sufficient to answer that it is all a question of tone unless one weighs the implications of 'tone' and realizes that one's 'answer' is indeed a 'question', a begging of it.

It may be that in forwarding a neglected aspect of poetic creation, I have pressed it to the point where it barely escapes becoming heretical. I am indeed half-persuaded by those who urge that the origin of a poem lies not in sound but seeing. Yet, if that is so, then the nature of the perception will depend, as far as the readers or—better—listeners are concerned, on the nature of that sound which communicates the perception. And as far as the poet is concerned—well, what he perceives and the way he does so may be conditioned by his obligation to communicate what he perceives in sound. But the whole problem is too complicated to allow of easy solution, or perhaps of a solution at all. I am aware that all I can have done in *Poetry and the Physical Voice* is but to contribute towards a discussion.

The poets and dramatists chosen for special enquiry have been considered in anti-chronological order for reasons given near the end.

It will be apparent that Mr T. S. Eliot's lecture, *The Three Voices of Poetry* (Cambridge, 1953), early provided a basis for my own speculations.

While specific obligations are acknowledged in the text, I would here thank those friends and colleagues whose interest has been generally helpful. These include: Miss Inga-Stina Ekeblad, who discussed the book in its preliminary stages; Professor G. Wilson Knight, who generously gave his encouragement and interest throughout; Professor Lewis Horrox, who has benevolently watched proceedings; and Dr Donald Davie, who early offered some acute practical advice. Yet none of these should be held responsible for the use I have made of their kindness.

Finally, I have to thank my wife for unremitting toil in the preparation of my manuscript and for enthusiastic readiness to talk over problems relating to the book as they arose.

F. B.

Sheffield.

PART ONE

INTRODUCTORY

... features may alter with the play of a private passion, but a voice is apart from these. It lies nearer to the racial essence and perhaps to the divine; it can, at all events, overleap one grave.

E. M. FORSTER, *The Longest Journey*

I Problems of Hearing and Saying

i

WHAT vocal sound does a reader hear, with his inner ear, when he silently 'peruses' a poem or passage of poetry? If what he hears corresponds with the actual physical voice of the poet, how does the poet create this awareness of his personal voice in the mind of the reader, a voice which the reader must— presumably—imitate, or attempt to imitate, when he renders the poem, or the passages of poetry, aloud?

This book is an effort at answering the question together with the cluster of related questions that arise: What is inward hearing and saying? What is aural empathy, that is, where, despite actual silence, there is present an illusion of vocal sound? Further, if a reader thinks he could voice aloud, say, *l'Allegro* satisfactorily (say it aloud so that what he says corresponds with what he heard when he perused the poem silently), but not *Paradise Lost*, Book VII, what does this imply? Does it mean that when Milton came to compose *Paradise Lost* his voice had changed since *l'Allegro* and that this reader thinks he can imitate Milton's earlier voice but not his later? Did Milton's voice change, and is the development of his style the evidence of this vocal change?

If so, does what happened to Milton happen to men generally? Do men's (if not women's) voices *change* (or develop new capacities to the loss of others) during the course of their lives? Is it general that a man, granting he has this gift for aural empathy, can approach to a satisfactory rendering aloud of *l'Allegro* when he is twenty-one, but will lose this ability at the age of fifty, and will gain instead a capacity to say *Paradise Lost*, Book

3

VII, as he thinks—or feels—it should be read aloud? Then, if poets' voices change during their lives like other men's, how is this indicated and reflected in their work? Against this, have not the poets, irrespective of their age in years at the time of writing, written in voices other than their own? Undeniably they have imagined voices, and spoken through or with these imagined voices. But is not this last question more pertinent in considering a dramatic poet like Shakespeare (who nevertheless wrote in his own changing voice in the *Sonnets*), or a narrative poet who uses characters, such as Chaucer (the Prioress tells us a tale in a voice that is distinct from that of the Miller when he tells his tale), than a lyrical poet who, using the first person singular 'I', mainly writes ostensibly in his own voice—Keats or Tennyson? Thus if Tennyson wrote plays of only limited success is it perhaps because he could not write with conviction for voices other than his own?

While these questions depend on our main question, other questions follow in connection with any possible findings. Thus: if a young poet begins his career by writing in some admired voice not his own, what sort of an achievement does this discovery of his own voice at last represent? Or: if an original poet is largely or wholly identifiable by his possession of a hitherto unheard voice (his own), how is the reviewer, spoken to in this voice, likely to respond? Pressed for time, is he not likely to say 'this voice is not my own, nor those of my colleagues'? And if he cannot reproduce this original voice, that is, say the poetry, as it ought to be said, aloud, is he not likely to dismiss it, both voice and experience? Remembering the history of Hopkins this seems a possibility. This raises another question: if this reviewer knows and accepts the voices of his colleagues, does not this argue the existence of 'group' voices—recognizable collective voices, hierarchical or sectional, belonging to particular occupational groups in place or time? I do not intend here to refer to the speech of social classes, for I point not to differences of vocabulary or 'accent' but the differences of voice, and the voice of *The Times* is distinct from the voice of *The Observer*. Yet in so far as vocabulary, the idiosyncratic preference for some verbal forms over others, is an aspect of voice this last question leads us to questions concerning dialects: concerning American, say, or Irish forms of English and their effect on the American or Irish voice; and to questions concerning the nature of sound and of poetry itself.

And here we touch certain finalities. One is that all poetry, with but few, and then recent, exceptions, is primarily sound[1] (and but secondarily meaning, meaning conveyed by or through sound) whether or not recorded in mute manuscript or print; and next, that poets, more so than all or most other people, have a peculiarly physical or passional awareness of vocal sound. That they are interested, even absorbed, by rhythm and meaning is consequent rather than precedent. In their poetry (the same observation applies, if only to a lesser extent, to a preacher like Donne or an orator like Burke) they live or endure a series of vocal sounds (and all the distension of being forced by the seemingly simultaneous, and yet really consequent, semantic energy released by such sounds) which we, as readers, echo. That is their life. How others live—for whom uttered words are cheap—is another matter.

This last statement may seem defensive or offensive or aggrieved. It is meant to be none of these but to urge forward a truth which ought to be recognized but which tends to be occluded by a discussion of the difference between 'semantic' (or 'discursive' or 'rational') and 'emotive' (or 'imaginative') language. The present suggestion is that there is one kind of language and another kind of language; and that the existence of these two kinds of language is only broadly serviceable to adduce in the old argument concerning the difference of poetry and prose since the *formal* difference between two kinds of composition does not coincide with the difference between the two kinds of language. Following a perception of two kinds of language, we would transfer certain kinds or examples of prose (e.g. Donne's *Sermons* or parts of them) into the category which includes most poetry and transfer some kinds of poetry (or some poems), which have already been settled to be no more than verse (though it can be good, even 'great' verse), into a category which it should share with the bulk of prose. Language can either be a do-er, an 'agent', or 'used' as an instrument.

[1] Real or imagined—imagined when, silently reading, we yet hear the voice of the poet. The assertion *poetry is primarily sound* is not, of course, made here for the very first time. The distinction belongs, I think, to Sidney Lanier: see *The Science of English Verse* (New York, 1909), pp. 21–24.

Referring to language as apprehended, and then expressed, by poets, in an essay published some time ago, I wrote that the poet 'knows linguistic sound in a special and obsessively physical way. He feels it with his whole body, almost as though it were a pervasive substance—inward bread as much as outward wine or air or communicative sound waves.'[1] This was a thickened and partly metaphysical way of trying to say something which must now be reduced to intellectual analysis in support of the premise that in poetry language is agent and not instrument. But it is easier to settle with language as instrument first.

When theorists of language (Otto Jespersen was one, but there are many others) consider language 'as an instrument for expressing thoughts',[2] or when logical positivists assert that words are 'tools' for the communication of ideas they may be— unfortunately *are*—right with respect to the overwhelming mass of word traffic that passes daily, year in year out, whether in conversation or print: think of women over tea-tables, men at a board meeting, of newspapers or official reports. But, outside such boring chatter, language is still only being *used as a means* in the great majority of books, whether the books are meant to entertain, such as novels, or to instruct, such as manuals of literary history or economics. In all such, language is a mere *means*, even if the purpose of the writer is hortatory and even if words are sometimes used to arouse the readers' emotions. Usually, in this traffic, whether spoken or written, one must concede that the means are trivial and the ends unimportant: people talk of the weather (the instrument) in order to be (or seem) sociable; newspapers are filled with words because the columns must be filled (the end); but sometimes instrumental language can be interesting, worthwhile or significant, e.g. the works of St Thomas Aquinas or a declaration of war.

By contrast with language as an instrument, language as an agent, the language of poetry and of some prose, is hard to

---

[1] *Books*, no. 308, March 1957. But Valéry, and I dare say others, have put it much better. Valéry insisted that his poetry was experienced as physical sensation (see Francis Scarfe, *The Art of Paul Valéry*, Heinemann, 1954, pp. 54, 60, 80). But then he explicitly conceived of his work as vocal sound, whether exerted by himself or from the bodies of others, as in *la Jeune Parque*. (*Ibid.*, p. 183, see p. 183n. below.)

[2] Otto Jespersen: *Language: its nature development and origin* (Allen & Unwin, 1954), p. 433.

define and occasionally difficult to recognize. By 'agent' we meant that the language is not *used* here as a means. Nor, when we meet it, should we try to get out of it what we try to get out of instrumental language—information or ideas. It is not subordinate to an end but is an end in itself. A poem is composed of active language, but the language in the constitution of a poem *is* the experience: the poet in writing creates his experience in the act of making the poem. And since poetry is of active language, which is vocal sound, the poet's sensation of language is a specifically intimate, passional, nervous and somatic one. For this theory of language as agent—involving a special kind of apprehension of vocal sound by the poet (or, put another way, he is *possessed* by vocal sound as a man was said to be possessed by devils—though to outward appearance this possession may be as fitful in the one case as it might have been in the other)—assumes that in the act of silent composition a poet is as physically worked upon or modified by what he writes as though he had composed aloud.

That this view of language—that it is either agential or instrumental according to whether or not it is apprehended vocally, i.e. originally experienced as vocal sensation—cuts across, rather than fortifies, the older division of language into two kinds according to whether its function is referential (or propositional or notional) or emotive (or evocative) is probable since, in deciding whether this or that piece of language is agential or instrumental, our test relates not to function but to origin.

Mrs Susanne K. Langer, in her attempt to establish that poetry is not necessarily oral,[1] asserts that 'the treatment of poetry as physical sound comparable to music' rests on an 'utter misconception'. She grants that there is some poetry 'that profits by, or even demands, actual speech', but claims that 'the voice of a speaker tends to intrude on the created world' and that 'very sonorous or musical poetry' is 'the easiest to "hear" inwardly'.

While it would be hard to deny that poetry in its origins was essentially a spoken form, or that the entire dramatic work of Shakespeare was designed to be heard, Mrs Langer's arguments

[1] Susanne K. Langer: *Feeling and Form* (Routledge & Kegan Paul, 1953), pp. 277–279.

have some force applied to a deal of recent poetry—eye-and-mind poetry, which is as silent as the numerical language of mathematics. They have an equal force when a poem is read aloud and the 'voice of a speaker tends to intrude on the created world' for the reason that the voice of this particular speaker is alien to the voice of the poet, is alien to the voice the poet had imagined. Thus if an old woman recites the speeches of Hamlet or of Claudius, or a young girl recites 'Crossing the Bar', listeners would be aware of an intrusion—the intrusion of the speakers' voices. What we rather ask of a speaker is that he lose his own voice in the voice of Shakespeare's characters or in Tennyson's, who is the 'character' or 'I' of 'Crossing the Bar'. The verse of Hamlet's speeches and the verse of 'Crossing the Bar' reveals not only how they should each be respectively modulated by a voice but also reveals the kind of voice necessary for these particular acts of modulation.

But when Mrs Langer goes on to say that 'very sonorous or musical poetry is the easiest to "hear" [*sic*] inwardly', the difficulty is to know what is meant by ' "hearing" inwardly'. That an 'inner ear' exists, no less than an 'inner voice' is certain though neither anatomist nor psychologist can tell us precisely what they are. They would seem not to depend entirely on memory. We know that the inner ear exists because it is the organ which allows us to hear Tennyson's voice when we silently peruse his poems, or—come to that—to know that poetry is rhythmical apart from the visual evidence of its typographical arrangement on the page. This inner ear allows us to identify Tennyson's voice in any one poem from our having learned to recognize it from our inward hearing of it in other poems. Now some poets might be content if their work were only inwardly heard because of their knowledge that their own voices cannot be reproduced by others with absolute precision. But this only applies to a few recent poets and cannot invalidate the rule that poetry is essentially a spoken form, even if some poems best speak, and are best heard, in apparently strict silence.

ii

Our enquiry will require the use of terms, some of which are used both with a loose variable meaning and a strict meaning. To avoid misunderstanding I shall here note these terms and give my own meanings, whether or no these agree with general or special definitions.

Pitch By pitch I intend, as the *Shorter N.E.D.* has it, the 'degree of acuteness or graveness of tone', or the degree of height or depth of voice when measured against a scale. 'Height' and 'depth', thus used, are, of course, metaphors:[1] but so also is 'pitch', literally a throwing or fixing. The *N.E.D.* illustrates with a vivid quotation of 1867: 'screaming out . . . in every conceivable key and *pitch* of shrillness.' Pitch, all would agree, is an essential and inalienable property of every single sound, whether vocal or otherwise. Pitch can be scientifically measured by means of the oscillograph which records the number of vibrations per second. The higher the pitch the greater the number of vibrations in that time unit.

Duration By duration is meant the length of a sound, its continuance in time. (A single sound *could* be infinitely continued.) A speech sound during its life can alter its pitch, return to the pitch of its starting and then cease. If Marvell's line

> Had we but World enough, and Time . . . ,

not only seems but is shorter than Crashaw's metrically identical

> Love, thou art Absolute sole Lord . . .

it is because the sum of the durations of the sounds of the latter line, together with any intervals or cessations from sound, is greater than the sum of the durations of the former plus its intervals, and requires a longer time if it is said as it ought to be said.[2] The series of vowels and diphthongs of Marvell's line

---

[1] For no real verticality is involved, though psychologically there may seem to be. Hence the scale. But the ancient Greeks aligned their scale, I believe, so that the 'low' notes were at the top and the 'high' notes at the bottom.

[2] 'We doubt whether, in the eighteenth century, could be found two poems in nominally the same metre, so dissimilar as Marvell's *Coy Mistress* and Crashaw's *Saint Teresa*; the one producing an effect of great speed by the use of short syllables, and the other an ecclesiastical solemnity by the use of long ones.' T. S. Eliot, 'The Metaphysical Poets', *Selected Essays* (Faber, 1932), p. 271. Consonants like vowels *take time* to sound, but the time to sound a vowel can be variably extended or shortened.

take less time to say than the series of vowels and diphthongs in Crashaw's, the pauses apart, even though the two series are numerically equal. Moreover there is a relation here between *duration* and *pitch*. The saying of Marvell's line is not only done more quickly than Crashaw's, but it is said (we feel) more lightly, or at a higher pitch. Other things being equal, the higher the pitch the more rapidly a series of sounds can be said.

Volume Volume refers to the degree of loudness of a sound. Volume can be scientifically measured in decibels. If a reader attempts to render a poem aloud, his control of volume will be related to two considerations. One will be the actual physical setting of his rendering and his actual audience: the size and shape of the room, the size of the audience, his relative nearness or distance from that audience. The other will be the nature of the audience and its physical setting imagined or assumed within, or by, the poem. In *To his Coy Mistress*, Marvell is an 'I' addressing a 'thou', an audience of one. The 'thou' is a girl with whom Marvell would have prompt sexual intercourse. He persuades to that end in his poem. We *over*hear but would of course be *de trop* as auditors or spectators. The audience of the poem will affect a rendering of the poem before an actual audience. By contrast, Crashaw's *Hymn to St Teresa* is public and ceremonial. The poem assumes a vast and splendid congregation. We join the congregation under the splendour of a baroque roof. Crashaw's line should be said more gravely and sonorously than Marvell's before an actual audience to suit the supposed audience of the poem.

To point a stronger, even gross, contrast. The volume of sound required by Donne's

> I Wonder by my troth, what thou, and I
> Did, till we loved?

whether for its imagined original audience or for a rendering before a modern audience, is small. Donne is speaking in a hushed whisper to a girl in the privacy of a room; or perhaps they are in bed. A 'revival' before a modern audience will be louder than the original utterance but should be no louder than is needed for hearing.

On the other hand:

> Hung be the heavens with black, yield day to night:
> Comets importing change of Times and States
> Brandish your crystall Tresses in the skie,
> And with them scourge the bad revolting Stars,
> That have consented unto *Henries* death.
>
> (I *Henry VI*, I, i, 1–5)

is not only stage poetry, something meant to be heard, despite the bad acoustics of The Theatre (The Globe constructed in 1599 of the dismantled timbers of The Theatre seems to have had different—and superior—acoustic properties[1]), but is Shakespeare (or someone else) remembering Marlovian strains and 'threatening the heav'n with high astounding terms'.

But though the real or assumed volume of vocal sound required for the rendering of poems is almost infinitely various, ranging from the loud roaring of the enraged Antony to the barely audible passages of soliloquy in *Hamlet* or the *sotto voce* of *The Love Song of J. Alfred Prufrock* (the term 'song' being ironic), yet since all poetry *is* sound, volume is implied in its rendering.

Timbre Timbre—no less than pitch, duration, volume—is an essential and ineradicable property of any and every sound, vocal or otherwise. But unlike its pitch, duration and volume, a sound's timbre cannot be scientifically measured or objectively described. The timbre of a sound must be imaginatively or subjectively described, e.g. if someone says a voice is metallic, it sounds like metal to a hearer. Or metaphors are employed to define a timbre, e.g. a 'warm' voice, 'astringent' tones.

It is a fact that the voices of no two people are, have been, or can ever be, alike. Even if two people produce a sound at the same pitch and for the same duration, and if they give it the same volume, yet the sound each makes is unique, and the short explanation of this is that the total complex of speech-organs of no two persons is exactly alike. It is this anatomical—indeed genetic—individuation which governs the timbre, and

---

[1] See below, pp. 150–152.

it is the timbre which gives any voice its specially distinctive quality.[1]

Now the specific timbre of the voice of a dead poet can, it will be maintained, sound from behind the pages of his works. That timbre, because it is unique, will be indescribable except by metaphor. But all who know the particular poet or poets would generally agree on the choice of a metaphor. Thus it would be agreed that Milton's voice tends to 'harshness' and that Keats' voice is 'mellow'.

From this it would seem to follow that no verse-speaker could hope to render aloud a poem in the precise timbre in which it was conceived and transmitted by its writer. Whatever the reader offers will be something other than what the poet gave and knew. Not that it is always easy to determine the timbre of the voice of the writer of a poem. But in truth the discovery of the timbre of a poet's voice is a major part of our experience of any poem, even though our description of that timbre has to be subjective.

If we have not discovered the timbre of a poem (not, now, poet), then we have not yet experienced it. In describing timbre we have to use subjective terms. Very well. But no one could assert that the opening lines of *The Canterbury Tales*, which are in Chaucer's own voice, had, when sounded, other than a soft or pleasing or winning timbre, or that the timbre of much of the later Milton was other than harsh. But besides these individual timbres we also have to recognize the group timbre of the poems of a period and place: the timbre of the American railroad ballads, or the timbre of the Irish folk-song, are those in which the idiosyncracies of the individual voice of the original writer and performer are submerged into those of his ethnic group, or region, or both. The larger classification exists: for independent of 'accent' or intonation, has not the American Middle West voice, no less than the West Indian negro voice, a recognizable timbre? All Americans of the Middle West may sound alike to strangers. Yet within the collective timbre of the Middle West is to be found the specific timbres of individual American poets differing from each other, yet united

[1] It strengthens rather than weakens my argument to point out that there are familial voices, that—for example—a mother and daughter, or brother and sister, can have voices recognizably akin.

by a timbre which differs from the timbre of the American South.

While every isolated vocal sound has four characteristics—pitch, duration, volume, timbre—of which only the first three can be objectively measured (and are expressive of a particular situation, mood or intention, while timbre is involuntary and is the result of heredity, though it can be altered by biological growth, accident or surgical operation), the next term only has meaning in relation to a series of sounds. Like timbre, *intonation* signifies a quality which can be felt and subjectively described but not objectively measured.

Intonation We might begin by saying that intonation is the result of the combination of pitches, durations and volumes, exercised in a series and subject to an overall timbre. Does a series of sounds, as distinguished from an isolated sound, suppose a will, and therefore a human intention?

The word 'intention' can mislead if we confine its meaning to 'conscious purpose', because much, even most, of what we intend is unknown to ourselves until it is said—though, when it *has* been said, the intention is conveyed through a series of sounds creating an intonation. Yet it would be equally wrong to substitute 'motivation' for 'intention' and refer 'motivation' to the areas of a person's being that he does not know about consciously. The border-line between conscious and unconscious, within a personality, is not fixed. The line is continually moving. In various conditions, moods, at different hours of the day or night, at different stages of life, a person can lose consciousness of his ownership of large or small areas of himself and can thereby forget his ability to employ those powers which such areas command. Nor does the line (to maintain the system of metaphors) only *rise*. At other times, the line lowers and the man then knows more of himself. And since the ever-moving border-line does not demark *abruptly* consciousness from unconsciousness, day-lit room from dark well—instead on each side of the line there are distensible or shrinkable zones of semi-consciousness (or semi-unconsciousness)—it will be appreciated that when we suggested *intonation* assumes intention, then the word 'intention' must not be narrowly interpreted.

Except for isolated cries of fear, anger, lust or triumph—which nevertheless have all to be related to a context if they are to have meaning—not single vocal sounds but a series of vocal sounds are required before a meaning can be conveyed; but since intonation, no less than meaning, requires a series of sounds, it follows that the intonation applied to the series can modify or colour the meaning of the series in a variety of ways. To illustrate: 'Where are you going?' can be intoned in a vast number of ways depending on variations in pitch, duration, emphasis (volume)—according to the speaker's 'intention' and situation—and timbre. Now every new intonation produces a different meaning, and each intonation depends on the situation—and each human situation, however much this fact is forgotten, is unique—yet when we came upon the line

'O where are you going?' said reader to rider,[1]

we heard it said as it had not been said before. The timbre of the author's voice gave the question an original intonation, and the timbre was all the stronger for the author's numinous feeling for Old English.

One would like to go one stage further and urge that serial linguistic sound, apart from the language issued from Whitehall and the like, which is purely functional and has never been apprehended vocally by author or typist but which is simply a mute sign language, must have intonation. For if one can recall a speech in a play, a line of dialogue in a novel, or even a line of verse which, from the context, is evidently intended to be uttered in flat or 'toneless accents', without intonation or melody (let us suppose the fictive speaker to be in a state of hopeless dejection), yet such a speech or line can only sparingly be used. It must then be *set against* intoned sound and achieve its effect as a purposed negative. The tonelessness of the line makes reader or audience specially conscious of the intoned sound of its context, and that intoned sound reacts on the toneless line or half-line (the speech can only be short) and gives it a 'reflected' intonation which it would not have in isolation.

Whether in literature or life, intonation can generally only occur when language is coloured by real or simulated emotion.

[1] W. H. Auden: *The Orators* (Faber, 1932). Subtract the 'O' and the intonation is altered.

If we consider some hackneyed expressions of the novelist, such as: 'He raised his voice in angry tones', or: 'She complained in sorrowful tones', or: 'In ardent tones he professed his love', or: 'In terrified tones she enquired of her child of each passer-by she met', etc., we note that in each case a primary human emotion (anger, grief, love, fear) is assumed to modify or colour the speech-sounds. 'Or colour': the metaphor reminds us that we can only describe (but not measure) intonation by reference to common human feelings, observations or perceptions, but that the words we use to describe are conditioned by *the listener*'s passions and prejudices which nevertheless he takes to be commonly held. If a man declares that another spoke in 'arrogant' or 'dignified' tones, he takes it for granted that what sounds arrogant or dignified to him would sound arrogant and dignified to all others.

Now when we enquire as to the intonation of Marvell's line

Had we but World enough, and Time . . .,

which is what a reader should therefore render or echo, we can see that this is controlled by the order of the first two words. Marvell knows, and we know—even if his Coy Mistress seems not to—that neither he nor ourselves have 'World enough, and Time'. By the simple device of inverting the two words 'we had' he expresses this—turning an Indicative statement of fact into a Subjunctive impossibility which we agree to pretend is a possibility.[1] This manoeuvre of Mood points to the relation between grammatical forms and intonation and pitch. If Marvell had written 'We had World enough, and Time', he would have stated a past fact, referred to opportunities he presumably neglected. The intonation would have been one of pure regret (if the opportunities were then indeed lost) or of partial regret and remembered satisfaction (if the opportunity was seized but was perfected and so is in the past affording no hope of re-enactment), and the pitch would have been considerably lower than the pitch needed in

Had we but World enough, and Time,

and because the pitch, something objectively measurable, of the words in the line that Marvell actually wrote is higher than the pitch of the one he did not, the intonation is proportionately

[1] For a fuller discussion of the poetic implications of grammatical forms, see my *Poets' Grammar* (Routledge, 1958), especially pp. 104–111.

lighter or, to avoid metaphor, gayer and more sophisticated. This example shows that different emotional moods require different grammatical constructions and that different grammatical constructions require different patterns of intonation.

Certainly, also, Marvell's first word 'Had' is not only said with the light tone appropriate to its Subjunctive Mood—conveying a meaning opposite to that if the two words had been in their normal order—and at a high pitch, but that the word receives a stress (possesses a volume of sound it would not bear in an Indicative construction) because of the stronger expiration of breath required. But the duration of the sound must be short. Moreover, the inversion 'Had we' has another effect on the sounding of the whole line: a longer pause before 'and Time' is required. This Marvell's comma, grammatically incorrect or redundant, marks.[1]

Crashaw's line

Love, thou art Absolute sole Lord . . .[2]

takes, as we said earlier, longer to sound than Marvell's, demands a considerably lower pitch and, because of the large auditorium in which Crashaw conceived it as being ceremonially heard, it needs to be sounded with *resonance*.

Overtones Overtones, in such phrases as 'ironic overtones', implying *meanings* to be inferred beyond those explicitly stated, has been a frequent word in literary criticism, since the 1930's. But I am not aware that the term has been used literally, as it is used literally in music criticism, to refer to vocal harmonics. Yet it is almost impossible to hear human speech without hearing, in addition to primary pitch, overtones.[3] Hence, in a study

[1] See p. 26 of H. M. Margoliouth's edition (O.U.P., 1927). Many modern editors, in correcting Marvell's punctuation, spoil his line. See, e.g., the quotation in T. S. Eliot's essay on Marvell (*Selected Essays*, p. 281).

[2] See *Sacred Poems* (1642), p. 317 of L. C. Martin's edition (O.U.P., 1927). When the poem was reprinted in *Steps to the Temple* (1646), the 'Author's friend' put the A of 'Absolute' in the lower case. But Crashaw wanted the syllable to bear emphasis.

[3] The writer here acknowledges his dependence on the standard authority on the human voice, V. E. Negus in his *Comparative Anatomy and Physiology of the Larynx* (Heinemann Medical Books Ltd., 1949); and also on W. A. Aikin's *The Voice: an Introduction to Practical Phonology* (Longmans, 1920) whose illustration on p. 53 of a Scale of Resonance is particularly helpful.

of poetry as essentially a phenomenon of sound, as something conceived in terms of the 'writer's' voice, which is recreated in the 'reader's' inner ear when he experiences verse, it is well to remember that 'overtones', literally understood, are inescapably relevant. Generally, the fuller the voice the greater the resonance, and the greater the resonance the more overtones. Crashaw's line, 'Love, thou art Absolute sole Lord', for example, because it assumes a large physical setting with a crowded congregation for its delivery, releases a much larger series of overtones[1] than does Marvell's 'Had we but World enough, and Time', which—said lightly and rapidly—will not employ the resonating cavities in the chest and head of the speaker to nearly the same extent. To make another and an extreme contrast: the overtones (harmonics) released in a correct rendering of almost any line from *Paradise Lost* are numerous and important; those released in an appropriate rendering of Edward Thomas' *Adlestrop* should be barely, if at all, heard by the listener: indeed it is on their near absence that the poem relies for its effect.

Register The difference between the light eager speaking of Romeo (independent of an actor's view of the part, the verse determines that the part should be spoken in this way) and the deep resonant speaking of Antony (similarly it is the phonology of the text that decides the question) can be attributed to the natural physiological change in the speech-organs of a man. A man's voice tends to deepen with age. His new powers of voice encourage him to use them and so create situations for himself which he could not have done years earlier. He may now have what is sometimes called 'a voice of authority'. This alters the speaker's personality (he adjusts his personality to conform with his deepened voice) and where Romeo had pleaded, Antony commands. Romeo has one dominant register for his speech, Antony another.

However the term *register* is difficult because phoneticians and

---

[1] It does when the line is delivered as quoted here, following the edition of 1642, published in Paris, which Crashaw himself superintended. In the posthumous edition of 1648 however, where the line reads 'Love thou art absolute, sole Lord / Of life and death', Crashaw's vocal intention is destroyed. The result of putting 'sole Lord . . . death' in apposition is to lower the volume and reduce the resonance of the initial statement.

musicians disagree as to its meaning. But it should be noted that if resonance is to be related to register it is only accidental, for register refers primarily to the range of pitch possible to a voice when the larynx is in one position rather than another and not to overtones.

If one sings (or whispers) the lowest note in the scale that one can manage and then ascends, there comes the point at which one must draw fresh breath and alter the position of the larynx before continuing the scale upwards. Singers may more or less successfully conceal this momentary break but they cannot avoid it. One may liken the operation to a driver changing gear from fourth to third as his car encounters an increasing gradient.

Now, in speaking up the scale, the same barrier, requiring a physical adaptation of the larynx for its negotiation, occurs as in singing. If a person says the line

Had we but World enough, and Time . .

in the mode that I have argued that it should be said, with all resonance eliminated except that created within the mouth, he will find that he cannot immediately follow it with a line requiring a full chest-resonance without first changing gear, i.e. effect a physiological adjustment of the larynx; and this demands a break in the sound, however much the break may be concealed.

The register employed for the singing of the top notes of the scale or for the saying of Marvell's line, I shall refer to as the top register. The other, employed in the saying of nearly the whole of *Paradise Lost*, where there is chest-resonance, I shall refer to as the low register. Beside these, there is the middle register of normal speech when resonance is generated not from the lungs, nor yet from the nasal cavity, but from the pharynx.

Linguists would add to top, middle and lower register, a fourth—the falsetto. This is not without its importance to English poetry when we remember Chaucer's Pardoner, Shakespeare's Flute, Sir Andrew Aguecheek, the whores in *Pericles*, or much of Shelley!

iii

We have been contemplating speech of any kind as an 'I-outwards' creation; and as an action performed by the speaker's mind and by his body. By exceedingly intricate movements of muscle, nerve, bone and blood the mind delivers its intention: an action of sound. Speech is significant vibration of the air produced by mind and body, though I dare say that behind mind and body, compelling their joint action, is a third factor, an X, for which the English word used to be 'soul'. But the 'I' that speaks usually means to be heard, and the speaker's voice will vary not only according as to *what* it says but also according to *whom* it says it, and even *where* it has to say it. (The voice, where 'intention' and the 'soul' are in doubt, has a certain autonomy best indicated by 'it'.) That is, the manner of a voice at any one moment is controlled by the listeners and the surroundings as well as by the speaker—unless indeed the speaker is, as the idiom forcibly has it, 'beside himself', speaking 'without regard to person, time or place', and as though not from within his body but from outside.

Language is heard as well as said. But it is outside our purpose to go into the physiology of hearing, and we merely note in passing that the ear is capable of hearing a range of sound vibrations that is vastly greater than is in the power of any human voice to make: in fact, the range of the voice hardly exceeds two octaves.

Reverberation Rather than the physiology of hearing we need now to consider acoustics and to recall that a poet, writing a public kind of poetry, will pitch his voice with respect to the size and shape of the room he is to be heard in as well as with respect to the size and constitution of his audience. For a voice not only resonates within the body of the one who is speaking (causing overtones) but it consequently resounds within the enclosed cubic space where the speaker stands. This is *reverberation*.

As light-waves from a naked electric-light bulb radiate in all directions so do unobstructed sound-waves radiate from the source of their creation. Unobstructed: for, if a speaker's head is turned from his audience, the sound-waves, which should be transmitted in the direction where they are most needed to be received by the ear clearly, are obstructed by the speaker's head. Therefore a speaker needs to face his audience not only that he may see them, but that they may hear him. This is so obviously well-known that I am ashamed to mention it but for the principle it illustrates, and for the purpose of glancing at a perennial difficulty confronting any theatre-in-the-round, viz: that however much a player may considerately address points on a circle through all the 360 degrees, there must always be one or another sector or segment of his audience which must receive the speech of that player obstructed, or receive it reflected, if it hears it at all. But before going on to reflection, we should remember that it takes time for sound-waves to travel (2,000 feet per second), and that the back rows of an audience hear what has been said after the front rows have heard it. We might also remember that no voice ever speaks disembodied, or suspended in the exact centre of a sphere; hence in practice the sound-waves of a voice speaking in a room encounter different points of obstruction at different moments of time. Moreover, just as light-waves, radiating from a naked electric-bulb suspended in a room, are refracted by the surface of walls, floor and ceiling against which they obliquely strike, so sound-waves —radiating from their source—ricochet from those walls, floors and ceiling which obstruct the continuation of their outgoing progress. Each sound-wave rebounds from the obstructing surface at the angle at which it struck it (as a ball bounces back from a flat wall at an angle corresponding to the oblique angle at which it is thrown) and will continue to rebound, in the same way, from the encounter of each further obstruction until its original force has expired. Hurl a ball in a fives court and note the sequence of rebounds it makes until all the movement that once originated from your hand and arm is lost; or hurl a rubber ball within the six-sided box that is a bare room and watch (if quick-sighted enough) its angle-making—though ever slowing—career until it lies quiescent, and one has a fair idea of *reverberation.*

What we have said is clearly highly relevant to all kinds of public poetry, but it will be equally clear that we have simplified the scientific facts intensely and in at least three particulars: (i) it is doubtful whether the cessation of a sound-wave would be reached so soon as our homely examples suggest, (ii) when a sound is created there is not a single wave started (though there may be a single ball used in a bouncing game) but myriads, and (iii) the number and quality of rebounds or reverberations will depend not only on the size and shape of the room but also on the reverberative qualities of the speaker's voice and the number and degree of intensity of reverberative components in his words. For some sounds reverberate more than others. Generally, those that resonate most strongly within the speaker's body reverberate most strongly outside: oo [u:] or ou [au as in loud] not only resonate but reverberate more powerfully than i [i], though this too depends—partly on the size of the room (in the smallest room of the house, as they smugly and snugly put it, i might reverberate more distinctly than u:)—and partly on the material (fabric) of which the walls, floor and ceiling of the room are constructed, or with which they are overlaid.

But the walls of a hall, a room or of a theatre absorb or transmit (in the act of reverberation) only certain frequencies of a particular sound-wave. In the last half-century or more architects, in league with engineers and physicists, have given their best efforts to discovering which materials and inner-linings most reduce reverberation (this, in fact, means finding the materials which absorb—do *not* rebound—all the lower frequencies of sound-waves) in auditoria, thereby making it impossible to hear the poetry of Milton or the music of Beethoven as fully as they were respectively conceived by their makers as being heard. Not finding materials which absorb all frequencies, these architects (with the approval of public bodies) aim to line all places of audition with stuffs which at any rate delete from the original sound all the lower frequencies. If Tennyson cannot be fully heard nowadays it is largely because, when he is recited at some festival or other, a large proportion of his essential sound is deducted by absorbent surfaces.

Now if acoustic engineers have wadded the walls of auditoria in order to assist the rapid delivery and reception of a light and thinned-out prose, or of a verse that is no more than an attenuated speech metrically patterned, what are we to think of the introduction of microphone and amplifier? The microphone deletes certain frequencies; the amplifier distributes what is left of a voice not lifted or intoned beyond what is called for in ordinary conversation. Such a mechanized distribution of poetry (whether in a hall or over a broadcasting system) might be favourable to the performance of some kinds of drama, as Sir Herbert Read suggests in an interesting essay,[1] or to the performance of some intensely private lyrics (where the writer seems to be speaking from within his last reserves), but it forecloses the effective realization in sound of all that body of poetry where inward resonance and outward reverberation is substantive, was a major part of the experience in its original creation.

Non-reverberative spaces and electronically distributed sound also prevent the effective re-creation of Elizabethan drama—that is, prevent the plays being heard as they sounded within the minds and bodies of their authors, original players and audiences.

It must be fully and frankly admitted, of course, that no one of us can ever hope to determine the reverberative properties of the Elizabethan, as we might of the Greek, theatre: no Elizabethan theatre survives, some Greek theatres remain or have been restored. But inferentially, from a study of Elizabethan dramatic verse (and prose), and from a careful 'inner'-listening to it, we can know or discover much. From such a study we could determine, even if we were not assured such was the case on other grounds, and from other records, that Lyly's dialogue was written to be spoken by high-pitched, clear-carrying, but not resonating voices of trained boys in a roofed-over hall with little or no reverberation (the dialogue is apprehended as being spoken with lightness, grace, point, wit and delicacy). By contrast, the verse of *Tamburlaine* or of *Henry VI* infers two public open-to-the-air theatres of strongly reverberative properties. The 'heavens', or overhead sounding-board, may have been deliberately used as an echoic instrument by Alleyn when he cast back his head to utter such a 'high-astounding term' as

> Set black Streamers in the firmament
> To signifie the slaughter of the Gods,

or by the rival at the rival theatre with his

> Hung be the heavens with black, yield day to night;
> Comets importing change of Times and States
> Brandish . . .

[1] 'Sotto Voce' in *The Tenth Muse* (Routledge, 1957), pp. 146–156.

and the fully end-stopped verse of Marlowe's and Shakespeare's verse can be explained as a practical need for the carry and fade-away of the resonance and reverberation generated by the 'mighty line'. And certainly it was in the quieter soliloquies of *Faustus* and the quieter verse of the early comedies, that Marlowe and Shakespeare respectively came to practise a lifting of the end-stop. Shakespeare's earliest run-on verse probably represents an exploitation of a level (volume) of speaking below that which set the whole frame of the theatre resounding.

Echo Echo, I take it, is to reverberation in the laws of sound as reflection is to refraction in the laws of light: that is, it is a direct casting back to the speaker of the sound he has thrown out, not the sound which meets an obstruction at an oblique angle (a glancing blow) and then continues to ricochet. Echo is a return as a ball, bounced against a wall at right angles, returns to the hand that throws it. Echo, therefore, makes its single answer and is then silent; unlike reverberation (or, come to that, resonance) it does not continue a series of vibrations in ever decreasing frequencies. And we should remember that an echo is returned at a higher pitch than the sound which awoke it; the wall (or other obstacle) which it hits at right angles absorbs or devours the lowest frequencies.

The Elizabethans and the writers of the early seventeenth century, both dramatists and writers of lyrics, were greatly interested in *echo*. Beside the direct instances where the device is employed in plays and masques by Gascoigne, Lodge, Heywood, Dekker, Jonson, Webster, and in poems by Sidney and George Herbert,[1] there are the instances where the phenomenon of echo is alluded to, or where echo is invoked, as in *Comus*. Sometimes Echo is presumed to be awakened, and is therefore mimed, as in Spenser or Jonson, while in these lines of *Twelfth Night*:

> *Halloo* your [i.e. Olivia's] name to the *reverberate* hills,
> And make the babbling Gossip of the aire,
> Cry out *Olivia*.[2]

---

[1] See F. L. Lucas: *Works of John Webster*, Vol. II, note to Act V, sc. 3 of *The Duchess of Malfi*, where these examples are cited.

[2] I, v, 291–293, italics added.

we are reminded, or informed, that the last syllable of 'Halloo'
carries far because as many resonances as possible are being reduced to a single frequency (for the head is thrown back,
whereas with the mouth in its normal speaking position at near
right angles to the larynx, the resonances issue from one cavity
before they issue from the other, and then at a different frequency[1]) and that this is the condition for remote *reverberation* or
echo. No doubt, Viola-Cesario in delivering the lines suited the
action to the meaning, throwing up her head to call out both
'halloo' and 'Olivia', and the syllables I have italicized were
half-sung out so as to awake the reverberative properties of the
open-to-the-air Elizabethan theatre. Many similar vocal effect
are found in the poem-plays of Shakespeare (especially *The
Tempest*) and other Elizabethan-Jacobean dramatists and, if I
have digressed, it is to illustrate effects and variations of sound
which most recent drama and poetry tend to forget or ignore.
But in Milton, it may be said, the interest in echo (in *Comus* the
Lady's song to Echo, 'Sweet Echo, sweetest Nymph that liv'st
unseen / Within thy airy shell' employs precisely those verbal
sounds best calculated to arouse the Nymph to answer; in
Comus too are the lines

> airy shapes that syllable mens names
> On sands, and Shoars, and desert Wildernesses,)

is but one aspect of an all-absorbing or passionate preoccupa-
tion with sound—vocal, instrumental, natural, artificial. And
the interest of Crashaw in echo, as in all aspects of sound, is
scarcely less than Milton's. Then there is Marvell. His voice had
been light and gay enough in the first paragraph of *To his Coy
Mistress*, but it changes in the second paragraph simultaneously
with the change in grammatical Mood from Subjunctive to
Indicative. Then come the lines

> Nor in thy marble vault, shall sound
> My ecchoing Song:

[1] A phenomenon which Wilfred Owen exploits, whether consciously or
unconsciously, in his use of pararhyme. In

> it seemed that out of battle I esc*a*ped
> Down some profound, dull tunnel, long since sc*oo*ped

he is making a significant contrast of sounds each with a *double* resonance.

24

Why does it there *echo*? Well, it won't echo because the singer will be dead too, but it is within a 'marble vault' (earth-sunken, barrel-roofed) that a man (stooping, peering into, singing strongly enough into) could most successfully have aroused a ringing, and almost instantaneous echo. As with Milton so with Marvell, it is those sounds and sound effects which are paradoxically present only because of their stated absence (cf. the stated absence of martial sounds in the *Hymn on the Morning of Christ's Nativity*) which are the ones that ring most strongly in the systems of their authors. Hence the song which, we are told, will not echo, must *echo* (despite the denial) when one, who would read aloud, says

> Nor, in thy marble Vault, shall sound
> My ecchoing Song:

It is odd that few poets since the seventeenth century have used echo as a device. Only E. A. Poe and Thomas Hardy spring to mind; and Poe was ignorant of the fact that echo responded in a higher pitch than the original sound.

iv

I am not forgetting, of course, that it is not only the size, shape and acoustic properties of the room[1] which modify or control the voice of a poet. That voice will also be controlled by the audience in that room, its size and constitution. It will also be controlled by the poet's relation towards that audience. He has one relation when he tells a story (*Beowulf*); another relation when, speaking through actors, he shows them a drama; another relation when he declaims *at* them—speaking to his audience as 'you' or 'ye' (*Childe Harold*), etc., etc. I mention actual audiences, but I do not forget that most poets since 1820, or even before then, in default of an actual audience, have simply assumed one.[2] But even then—when an audience is merely assumed—the poet has had to adopt an attitude to it

---

[1] The general term is to include hall, theatre, chamber, etc., or even the dome of the sky where primitive ballad or *carole* are being considered.

[2] See, e.g. F. W. Bateson's *Wordsworth: a Re-interpretation* (Longmans, 1954), pp. 187–197, for a discussion of the audience Wordsworth assumed he was addressing aloud when he composed his poems.

and that attitude has controlled his voice. But all these considerations are better left to the time when we come to discuss the voices of some particular poets.

Finally, a man's voice changes with age. A man of fifty has a different voice than the one he possessed as a youth of eighteen or twenty-one. If he lives to be eighty it will have changed again. But though the changes are greater in some than in others, and though the objective measuring of such changes is difficult, they certainly occur. It will be remembered that in Jacques' famous speech, on The Seven Ages of Man in *As You Like It*, each Age has its characteristic voice, each presumably imitated in turn by Jacques. A study of such changes in a poet's voice is important for an understanding of his life's work.

II *Voice and Language*

i

I T might be questioned whether we have sufficiently realized
the intimate relation between voice and a language in the
various phases of its history. It might be objected that Marvell
and Crashaw would not have pronounced the words of their
lines as modern readers pronounce them; alternatively, that
Marvell's and Crashaw's seventeenth century pronunciation of
English affected their individual voices to a degree which makes
it difficult or impossible for a modern reader to imitate them.

This leads us to some general problems.

Is there such a thing as a 'national voice'? If it be conceded—
notwithstanding the plain truth that no two people can ever
have exactly the same kind of voice nor can speak exactly alike
—that there does exist an 'English voice' (or a 'French', or a
'German', or a 'Spanish', or an 'Italian'), a theoretical norm to
which each individual English voice can be referred, it remains
an open, and perhaps insoluble, question whether that national
voice is what it is (distinguishing it from a German or Spanish
voice speaking English howsoever well and fluently) *because* of
the language it employs (following the argument that the
habitual use of a language modifies the structure of the speech-
organs and so creates a peculiar type of voice), or whether the
voice is such as it is because of the genetic constitution of its
speakers. Is there, that is, a racial norm for the structure of the
speech-organs to which all Englishmen tend to converge?[1]

[1] Thus C. D. Darlington, in an article in *Nature*, would correlate those
speakers of languages which have the *th-* (th as in *this*) sound with those
geographical areas in which more than 40 per cent of the population belong

We have posited alternatives. But it seems more likely that it is not a question of alternatives. Rather: the habitual pattern of speech-sounds, as existent in any one language, taught by mothers and inherited over many generations, as much conduces to a typical national (in a large sense, tribal) voice as do biological factors. Thus, if there is a typical English voice distinct from a typical German voice, there is also a typical American voice. Speaking but a variety of English, the American's voice is yet distinct from the Englishman's. But that American variety, surely, is not to be attributed to *either* purely genetic *or* purely linguistic factors only. It is to be attributed to the interaction of both of these, and also to historical, geographical, climatic—and so psychological—factors, all combining to differentiate 'the American' from 'the Englishman' generally.

Nevertheless when a nation, which I would *like* to think of as a confederacy of related tribes, does make a major change in the constitution of the sound values of its language (for language, first of all, is vocal sound), then that change does argue a corresponding change both in the bodily structure and the mental disposition of the mass of speakers of that language in which the sound change occurs. It signifies a mutation. Thus, for example, the formation—we refer to a positive change even though the exact date of its occurrence will remain in doubt—of the characteristic English a [æ] as in *fat*, from West Germanic back aɪ, was one of the most dramatic, influential and, it would seem, final, events we have ever undergone. Almost equally important was the change whereby the aɪ in *stan* was fronted to become ou in *stone*; or the change whereby the aɪ in *slahan* (putative West Germanic) became ei in *slay* through fronting and loss of the intervocalic back *h* [x, as in loch]. These were early and definitive changes. They were created by the German invaders and settlers, or Anglo-Saxons, of this land within a century or two of their coming here, or they were created *on* them by the new surroundings and conditions. Whether these changes are regarded primarily in terms of loss or primarily in terms of gain

---

to blood-group A; and another geneticist points to an interbred community in Japan which habitually fails—and is unable to—express a particular sound common in Japanese.

(but wherever there is loss there is some gain, and *vice versa*), they must be regarded as dramatic events. They represent mutations of physical constitution and of consciousness, whereby the speakers became the less what they were—Germans—and the more what they are—English. (Corresponding linguistic events could be cited whereby the English colonists beyond the Atlantic became American.) We have instanced some particularly early changes. But linguistic change is a continuous process, which is to say that change in the speakers of the language is also continuous, even if the tempo of the process varies, so that over some periods (such as the eighteenth century) it is hardly discernible, while at other times (the time of Chaucer, of the Renaissance, the twentieth century) it is both rapid and extensive.

We have called attention to the basic element of a language, the single sound. But it is of course recognized that changes, or losses and gains, in single sounds are only part of the story. The peculiar quality of a national voice (and we certainly mean English and not British) is also modified by changes in vocabulary; by changes in patterns of intonation; by the emergence of new idioms and by the obsolescence of old, etc. The combination of all these go to make the English voice a register of national or, better, tribal experience. We would also claim that the personal voices of great poets, who also of course extend or develop the semantic resources of the language in the act of exploring and exploiting it, modify the national voice through their work which channels or records their voices. But enough has perhaps been said to make it clear that when we say that a piece of verse, composed three or four centuries ago, sounded such or such, we take into account those changes in English that have been recorded by historians of the language. We realize that

> wil ail greit neptuɪns ouʃein wɔʃ ðis bluɪd
> klein frum mi handz

as a norm of Jacobean pronunciation is something other than

> wil ɔil greit neptiuɪnz ouʃən wɔʃ ðis blʌd
> kliɪn fr(ə)m mai hæns

as a norm of modern pronunciation. Equally, we realize that Shakespeare, Burbage and every other Elizabethan sounded a departure from their norm since, as Whitman puts it, 'each existence has its own idiom'. But we also realize that Jacobean pronunciation can never be exactly determined beyond dispute, that individual timbre is more important than group pronunciation, and that what is chiefly important, for our present purpose, is how his language sounded within Shakespeare as he wrote it, how Burbage said it, and how the audience heard it: also to realize that Shakespeare's and Burbage's voices changed during their lives.

ii

But if we have been accepting as a truth that there is a standard English voice now, and that there was a standard English voice in the seventh century, and in the seventeenth, we should also mind the obvious truth that species of English voices exist in space no less than in time. Remembering that a language, and a voice which uses it, mutually modify each other, we refer to dialect voices (and the difference between dialect and language is merely one of kind, not of degree).

But, thus, under 'dialect' as a speech variant in space in modern time, we not only need to take into account the dying dialects of Hardy's or Barnes' Wessex or Clare's East Midlands but the usurping dialect of the U.S.A. 'Usurping', because the 'standard' is still London, England. But what if the 'standard' should change? Meanwhile the dying dialects of Burns, Clare, Hardy and Barnes protest their continued life in the poetry or the novels of these men.

What do we learn of 'dialect', and what of speech and of poetry, and what of humanity, through the poetry of these men —which will give their 'dialects' a life after other dialects have died?

Though Barnes conceived of and said,

> the blue hill'd worold,

or of

> The gookoo over white-weav'd seas
> Do come to zing in thy green trees,

in his own individual, and so strictly inimitable voice, yet that voice would have been kin to those of his whole dialectical group, a folk, a 'race' within a race. This inner 'race' would owe its voice to its specific climate, history, environment and genetic constitution. Thus if Barnes' dialect dies something else dies, a way of *knowing* and *feeling*, so that Barnes' own voice, and therewith that of his 'race' or folk, will become something to reconstruct with historical effort, a memorial act. And that is what one has to do for Shakespeare now—reconstruct his regional or dialectical and period voices, and, within these categories, his personal voice.

And yet timbre distinguishes a voice—individuates it—more than a dialect, for it is possible to distinguish a Norfolk voice from a Norfolk voice though they both speak dialect, or a Norfolk voice from a Somerset voice even though neither speak dialect. Suppose the Norfolk man and the Somerset man to have 'ironed out' their dialects, or that they belong to the class which would have bred out any dialect several or many generations ago, then though vocabulary, pronunciation, the grammar, the intonation of both speakers is faultless according to the standards of the spoken English of the southern public schools, the timbre of Norfolk and the timbre of Somerset will emerge as distinct, though whether a listener could place these two kinds of timbre would depend not only on his interest in the matter, and on his accuracy of hearing, but also on his topographical experience. Many might be inclined to attribute this difference of timbre not to voice but to difference of habits of mind, and might refer to the relative difference between pace and pitch of average speech among standard English speakers in Norfolk on the one hand and in Somerset on the other. This is plausible, for pace and pitch, in affecting the overtones of a sound, and of a series of sounds, might help to define the quality of a voice. But Dr Daniel Jones would rather attribute the difference between the two timbres in terms of phonemes; would argue that the difference is to be attributed to the physiological differences, however minute, of the speech-organs of the two speakers. And indeed, though mind and body seem to be inextricably involved in all functions, it would seem safe to suppose that the distinctive regional timbre of a voice—discounting, again, all questions of dialect—is due to the speaker's genes, that he shares the genetic constitution of the region in which his family has lived over generations. In fact a distinctive timbre can probably even survive emigration, even though it might be somewhat modified in time by an unconscious imitation of the phonemes of the region in which the emigrant settles. But that a regional timbre can be caught, momentarily assumed—perhaps mimicked—and conveyed in poetry, is shown by Chaucer. In the story of the Reeve in the *Canterbury Tales*, the peculiar timbre—or tang—of the East Anglian voice is caught (the East Anglian physical type and personality of the owner of that voice being thereby also caught) by Chaucer and conveyed above the poet's own characteristic and very different kind of voice.

We have been considering regional voices that have shed a dialect but preserved a regional timbre. Such a timbre may be indeed almost the only topographical individuality still possessed by a speaker of 'standard', or southern, or public-school, or BBC English. Whichever epithet is preferred, it is a class or caste English. Is such an English less tyrannical now than twenty years ago? If so, is it because the BBC, reacting against being teased, are now less keen on imposing on their announcers a house-style vulnerable to caricature as unmanly or affected? Or is it because the public, now owning television sets, watch more and listen less? Or because so many of the public, who resented BBC English in the 1930's, now speak BBC English themselves? Whatever the cause, and though myself born and bred to that caste English, I propose to mention briefly its danger—remembering that by BBC English we mean the BBC voice, a justifiable temporary equation if it is recognized that the adoption of any one manner or style of voice precludes the use of all those areas of vocabulary which would not suit that manner or style, and precludes the use of all those patterns of pitch and intonation consequent on—and appropriate to—those areas of vocabulary.

The obvious thing to say is that this English—compared with, say, Shakespeare's or any Elizabethan's—is narrow. Trying to use it ourselves now, we admit that it is but one kind of English voice and language. Used habitually, as instrument not as agent, by one kind of Englishman in all his public and private life, it follows that the owners of such a caste voice tend to exclude from essential recognition not only all those other voices employed by others, but all those aspects of themselves—

probably their most central or real ones—which demand another voice, if the speakers are to become even remotely their full selves. The rule of this caste voice on the mind, or from within the mind, of its speakers has this result: English poetry which was not originally spoken in the caste voice goes, though not unread, unheard.

III The Voice in Time

i

Most poetry is vocal sound (though not all vocal sound is poetry) and not the signs *for* vocal sound printed on a page; and though we suppose that modern poets compose silently, we also suppose that in composing they record what they are inwardly experiencing as vocal sound, usually their own voices however idealized. More completely, we could say they record the double experience of hearing *and* saying.[1] The more essentially a poet *is*, when he is composing, the more vocal sound (comprehending rhythmical impulse, metrical and stanzaic design, rhyme, cadence, etc.) is compulsively

[1] Up to about the time of James I *readers* framed with their mouths, and probably murmured *sotto voce*, all that their eyes saw on the page. The evidence usually cited for this is the early biography of Bacon. We might also remember that the Council of Trent enjoined priests, when 'saying' their daily Office in private, to actually frame the words of the Breviary with their lips: otherwise, it was held, the prayers were not effectually performed.

It might of course be maintained that this enjoinder suggests that priests, sharing a genuine trend among the educated, were beginning to byepass a stage—the stage of reconverting into sound what, in their case, had been originally conceived as verbal sound; that this enjoinder is to recall them from a practice that has now become universal among all readers except the barely literate—the practice of noting words as though they were Arabic numerals or inaudible advertisement signs. Obviously, this is no way to 'read' poetry, which, at the least, must be heard in the inner ear. But the general atrophy of the capacity to 'hear' what is seen on the page, an atrophy promoted by modern systematic education, is probably a main reason why so few people in the west now read poetry—or write it so as to be audible.

34

experienced as auditory and oral sensation. Even an image, conveying a mental picture, conveys its picture through sound: the sound is immediate, the picture mediate. For, if the phrase that the poet is experiencing at the moment—and clearly he is the first ever to experience it, if it is a genuine poetic phrase—is, or contains, a visual image, then that visual image, if not apprehended so, is yet transmitted, by him in terms of vocal sound, vocal equivalence. Indeed, if such an original image is not purely or merely visual but also appeals to, activates or involves other senses, or all the senses, attains even that happy intensity where the poet has, as it were, acquired the being of the thing of which he 'writes', yet still such a creation is expressed in, by or through vocal sound and nothing else. Nothing else, unless the poet is also a dramatist and is simultaneously setting something *physically* visible before his listeners' eyes.

To illustrate this in passing one turns first, though it is a law of all poetry, to Keats or Shakespeare. Let it be a phrase or two from Keats:

> And fill all fruit with ripeness to the core;
> To swell the gourd, and plump the hazel shells
> With a sweet kernel . . . ,

examples making us marvel once more at Keats' 'Identity . . . informing and filling some other Body' other than his own.[1]

Here he informs the bodies of the 'gourd' and the 'hazel shells', and their ripeness and sweetness are known as in the intimacy of physical union. The *einfühlung* is glorious and characteristic. Nevertheless (the word suggests one is about to deduct and one is doing nothing of the kind), nevertheless the impressions of 'filling', 'swelling', 'plumpness', of 'gourd', 'hazel shells', and the sensation of fruition and performance, are all alike realized in the medium of vocal sound, in the sound of Keats' own voice —here employing its most warmly mellow, grateful yet consigning tones. Such tones are unlike the thrilled, eager and

---

[1] *The Letters of John Keats*, ed. by Maurice Buxton Forman, (O.U.P., 2nd imp., 3rd ed. 1948), Letter 93, p. 228. I accept G. Beaumont's suggestion that for 'in for' Keats intended to write 'informing'. Yet Keats' slip of the pen makes perhaps the *richer* of the two readings.

lighter tones—when all was prospect instead of the contemplation of completion—of

> A laughing schoolboy, without grief or care,
> Riding the springy branches of an elm.[1]

for Keats' voice, like other men's, changed; and this brings us to the main concern of this chapter.

'Each existence has its own idiom', Whitman says with the beauty of precision. But 'idiom' properly—neither widely or narrowly, but properly—understood implies not only verbal forms, signifies not only what is said but how it is said. No two flowers are alike, each leaf has its *haecceitas*, and each person has his own voice. *What* any person says is almost always too common and too commonplace, a denial of individuality, but *how* he says it—try as he might to attune it to a caste or a class voice of the sort we have discussed—*will* have an individuality. And a poet, no less than other men, will have his own voice, try as much as he will to inhabit, become or be the voice of another or of others. Despite Keats, a poet in this is also a person, he 'has an Identity'.[2] Person. The word signifies a 'sound through', a 'mask to sound through'. More than other persons a poet is obsessed by 'persons', since he is a person obsessed, scored and spoored by vocal linguistic sound. One poet's voice inevitably differs from another's, however much he may echo that other's in his apprenticeship or immaturity. Yet, though his own, it will alter like other men's.

---

[1] From 'Sleep and Poetry' in *Poems 1817*.

[2] See *Letters of John Keats, op. cit.*, p. 228. That voices can be identified is beyond dispute, but *how* they are identified is a matter for discussion. J. N. Shearme and J. N. Holmes, in 'An Experiment concerning the Recognition of Voices' (*Language and Speech*, vol. 2, part 3), report that a number of speakers, using the same words in each case, were recorded on a tape. The idiosyncrasies of speech-rate, accent and even pitch were then eliminated. The majority of the panel of listeners continued to recognize the voices of the different speakers. The writers conclude that it was the 'spectral envelope' of each voice that was recognized. What is intended by 'spectral envelope' remains vague.

In the same number of *Language and Speech*, Yoshiyuki Ochiai, in 'Identification Studies using Japanese Vowels', reports an experiment whereby the speakers confined themselves to the utterance of five Japanese vowels. The listeners, he concluded, identified the speakers from their different timbres and not from their phonemes. (Phoneme is the term used to denote individual differences in the formation of a sound.)

Voices alter, and partly in accordance with the physical and physiological laws governing speech and hearing referred to in Chapter I. Partly, because there are certainly some non-physical and non-physiological conditions—not laws, for the conditions are not sufficiently known—which also contribute to such alterations. But let us consider the observable physiological changes first.

At puberty a boy ceases to be a boy, even though he is not yet a man. During that crisis, for it is a crisis more than a period (in the sense that boyhood and middle age are periods), his vocal cords lengthen with a relative suddenness. Likewise they broaden. It is true that since his infancy and before, indeed since his origin, his vocal cords had been growing steadily and at a rate proportionate to the growth of all his parts, but at puberty the growth is so speeded up as to produce a crisis. In a week or two, or in a few days—so I am assured by specialists of the subject—the voice 'breaks'. The man-boy's management of his new voice may be uncertain for a while, but he has already left childhood behind and, speaking with a new voice, he is forced to grow a new 'personality' to accompany it.

Now, of course, I am aware that this voice-change is one of several changes and that it accompanies a change in the sexual organs and is held to be secondary or auxiliary to that. But I am anxious not to be sidetracked. I think 'secondary' and 'auxiliary' can mislead. The voice-change is a social change that cannot be concealed. It is also the individual's private affair, and one of its results is that he notes the voices of other individuals as he had not done before. He notices women's voices. He can also hear poetry for the first time in tones he can refer to his own experience as a speaker. In effect, and in the terms of the physics of sound, he has lost the power to create a range of treble notes and has gained the power to create bass notes. But it is not only a question of pitch. Enlarged sinuses, larynx, chest cavity, means that the deeper sounds he now makes do, or can, *re*sound within himself. If he is to awake to poetry at all, as an experience central to him, it happens now. With the doubtful exception of Pope there are no infant prodigies in poetry as there are in music, mathematics or chess. A boy musician sounds through an instrument which he shares with grown players—a violin; a poet sounds with his own voice, which is not an instrument but an agent. Now women, with few exceptions, do not become poets. Nor do men with few exceptions. But the exceptions among men are far more numerous, 'infinitely' would be an almost justifiable overstatement, and I would explain this by saying that all men undergo the primary qualifying condition for becoming poets—however few proceed beyond that stage—and no, or few, women do. It is true that the vocal cords of girls also lengthen during their puberty, but this is usually experienced as a continued slight deepening of the voice and not a drastic change; as a continuation of a process rather than as a crisis. Not that women are therefore unable to read or hear poetry. Women readers and listeners of poetry probably excel in numbers men, for women can hear with more genuine interest the voices of men than they can the voices of their own kind. But when they read poetry by men, instead of both hearing and—as men at least ought to do since it is in their power to do so—vocalizing, albeit silently, the words, they hear only. Moreover, in the poetry of the very few genuine women poets, I believe that one can hear a female voice sounding through and behind the words.

I have been assured by some physiologists that the voices of men, once broken, remain unchanged until death. I do not believe it. Beside the evidence of some medical specialists such as J. Terracol[1] and phoneticians, there is the evidence of poetry and there is the evidence of common observation and of common experience. Shakespeare made such an observation, the truth of which one would have thought evident though it has been denied. Jacques speaks of the time of a man's life, when

> his bigge manly voice,
> Turning againe toward childish trebble pipes,
> And whistles in his sound.[2]

This observation would, it can be supposed, have the support of many who have listened to the speech of elderly men. Speaking involves the complex co-ordination of an immense number of muscles (as well as thought or feeling or both) distributed over a large area of the body. What wonder if the control exercised

---

[1] In (with R. Azemar), *La sénescence de la voix* (Largentière, 1949).
[2] *As You Like It*, II, vii, 161–163.

over such a co-ordination can be impaired or falter in old age. An old man's voice quavers, as anyone acting the part of an old man on a stage is made to learn. This is because not only the force of expiration of air from the lungs is reduced but the expiration is uneven in its force. The vocal cords lose elasticity and become calcined. Moreover, the voice can turn again toward 'childish trebble' for possibly psychological reasons. The old man is a pitiable object and he can unconsciously ask for pity; and anyone, whatever his age, making a plea tends to raise the pitch of his voice. This is why the self-pitying are said to whine.

We have mentioned the voice of a man at his puberty and in his old age. Between these extremes his voice has a history, and it is between these extremes that nearly the whole of significant poetry has been created though it is possible to detect the tremulousness in the voice of Tennyson in 'Crossing the Bar'. Now the usual course of that history is debatable. To generalize, where human beings are concerned, is only to provoke exceptions, for as 'each existence has its own idiom' no two existences have the same history. History is experience requiring time, and experience is that which modifies a personality, and so voice. But some, perhaps of deliberate choice, have little or no experience though their years are many. Moreover, even among those who have had undeniably much history, there is no standard rate for the succession of various phases of being. Keats, for example, on the strength of Middleton Murry's wonderful book,[1] underwent in five years what took Shakespeare at least fifteen. But there is no merit in rapidity of development— providing the man lives long enough—but only in development.[2] But if we do venture to construct a norm of the history of the male voice we must look for our data in poetry, for poets have chronicled their voices more fully and minutely than have others—except perhaps some orators.

I would say that poetry shows there is a difference between the voice of a man in the first flush of his youth and the voice of the same man in the height or fulness of his middle age. The

---

[1] *Keats and Shakespeare* (O.U.P., 1925).
[2] Indeed, Keats himself said: 'Nothing is finer for the purposes of great productions than a very gradual ripening of the *intellectual* powers.' *The Letters of John Keats*, edited by M. B. Forman (O.U.P., 1948), Letter 41, p. 88. But note the word here italicized.

proof of this lies in the fact that it has to be read aloud differently. I would say that the voice behind, or in, *Tamburlaine*, part I, which is generally dated 1587, is distinguishable from the voice behind *Edward II* (1592 or 1593); that the voice of Keats in the Odes of the 1820 volume is distinguishable from his voice in the 1817 volume; and that, apart from what it says, the voice of a stranger on the telephone reveals his approximate age—whether he is nearer fifty or eighteen; and that Marlowe and Keats made in four or five years a good part of the journey that takes others twenty or thirty years.

Of course, the voice of a stranger on the telephone (it is realized that the Post Office engineers have arranged that we hear only part of a human voice on the telephone; certain frequencies, certain overtones, that is, which exist in a 'live' voice are deleted in the act of transmission) tells us other things beside his age, however formal or perfunctory his message. The information about its owner which a voice can betray, besides age, includes (i) class or caste (within which 'collective' or norm, his own voice—however nearly it is assimilated to the norm by tone—yet has its undeniably unique existence) (ii) his intelligence, sensibility, education and training—and happily none of these qualities can any longer be directly related to social class: e.g. a red-brick graduate's voice can reveal its owner as having sprung from the lower middle or working classes even at the moment that it reveals a trained intelligence and sensibility, (iii) the part of the country, or of the world, from which he derives his genetic character and the cast of his personality—and this applies even if the voice speaks 'southern standard English'[1], though more so if it does not, (iv) his temperament and temper and so his occupation,[2] interests and his past (that these are less consequent than complicatedly intermodulatory in their influence, I recognize, but cannot give the space here for an analysis of proportions infinitely variable). Primarily, of course, after the sex we can tell the age, for much that we can tell beside is consequent on these two.

Now it would probably be generally agreed that the voice of a very young man can be distinguished from the voice of a very

[1] See p. 31, *supra*.

[2] There was a series of BBC programmes broadcast during 1959, entitled 'Occupational Voices'.

old man. Whether the voice between these two extremes either *does* or *can* undergo changes I am prepared to argue on the evidence of reading poetry and the experience of listening. But there are no absolutely objective tests available for establishing the truth of this. Or rather, the techniques for such tests exist but have not been applied in a laboratory.

ii

Experiment and common experience show that a man's voice continues to change during his lifetime, no less than the entire rest of his body and mind, after the dramatic 'break' at puberty. But when we come to consider the rate or pace of this change, and if we try to correlate this rate with other changes, we obviously find ourselves in difficulties—the sort of difficulties which prevent dogmatism. Shakespeare, in the *person* of Jacques, may speak of the seven 'acts' or ages of 'Man' but, clearly, any precise attempt at demarking of 'act' from 'act', or age from age, must offer difficulties. Some might urge that the vocal changes (or growth of the voice, or its development, or its decay—but it is all these) are so imperceptible as to make nonsense of Jacques' 'Acts' or ages; others would more properly assert that the rate of change is in no two cases the same. Granted, but does that make nonsense of Jacques'—and our—attempt to distinguish the voice periods of an individual in the way a historian distinguishes (on the broadest scale) ancient from medieval, or medieval from modern? Obviously it does not, and the reason why it does not is interesting.

Shakespeare-Jacques, or these poems and pictorial representatives of the 'Acts' or ages of life, tell us that the process of growing towards death is not necessarily so imperceptibly gradual after all; they tell us that the passage from youth to middle age, or from middle age to old age can seem—whether to sufferer or to observer—sudden. Sudden, though the exact year of life at which the passage is made across the line dividing one category of 'age' from another can widely vary according to the individual. Someone says, or it is said of him, 'that he grew old overnight', which may but slightly exaggerate the truth that change, though incessant, can build up a resistance which suddenly yields. Now the point of these remarks is that the state of puberty is not the only crisis in a man's life (taking 'crisis' to mean 'a lot that happens in a short time after a long—sometimes submerged, submerged to self-recognition—build-up'), but that other crises occur, hardly less dramatic (in the Aristotelean sense) than puberty: the departure from youth, or the departure from mature manhood. Next there is the more clearly relevant point: that with these later changes, as at puberty, there is a voice-change. This leads to the question: How are these voice-changes revealed in the poets?

An answer to this question is one concern of the rest of this book. Here we point out that if vocal changes are important to all people, who live to undergo them, they are likely to be especially important to poets since their occupation is with vocal sound.

But before considering the cases of individual English poets, there is one more question, with the widest human application, to put.

Granting that an aged voice can be distinguished from a just-broken voice, what are the nature of the changes occurring in between these?

Cautiously making due allowance for all the exceptions, I distinguish four periods in the history of a physical voice (a) the voice of the youth, (b) that of early middle age, (c) that of late middle age, (d) that of old age. Not many poets have produced through all four of these periods in their own persons, though Wordsworth and Tennyson immediately come to mind, but, in those who have, we note changes in grammatical structure and grammatical emphases accompanying the changes in vocal *sound*. For not only does the sound of a man's voice change at about thirty, and at about fifty, but the content of what he says also changes.

Now St Paul says, 'young men see visions and old men dream dreams'. He points to opposed grammatical forms as they express vision and memory. The characteristic grammatical Tense and Mood of the young is therefore the Future and the Future Subjunctive respectively—the Tense expressive of intention and the Mood expressive of vision and desire. These are in fact, as we will show, the characteristic inflexions of the voice of the young poet. The characteristic Tense and Mood of the aged is the Past Indicative and a Pluperfect Subjunctive—the emphasis depending on the degree to which original, or later substituted, desires or hopes have been accomplished ('lived', 'experienced') or frustrated of attainment. Now no one likes to acknowledge defeat and the aged voice of the poet is not necessarily as straightforward as in

> Footfalls echo in the memory
> Down the passage which we did not take
> Towards the door we never opened
> Into the rose-garden.[1]

but when these inflexions are not honestly owned to, they have to be detected by the *tone* of a voice which can belie what it says. Yet, on the whole, the few poets who have lived to write, and to speak, into old age are honest.

St Paul did not sum up the characteristic spiritual states or attitudes of the two periods of middle age. We can distinguish the physical voices of these two periods, but how is what they say differentiated? Both periods of life are on the whole concerned less with what might be, or what has been, than with what *is*. In the former, the impact of actual experience in friction with earlier 'hopes' or 'visions' leads to a tension between Indicative and Subjunctive that provokes the ironic voice. In the latter period, though the physical voice is the voice of late middle age, anything might happen in the substance of the poetry and so in the inflexions, inflexions grammatical and the inflexions of tone appropriate to those grammatical constructions. For the inflexions appropriate to a delayed satisfaction obtained at great sacrifice we can turn to *Antony and Cleopatra*. There are the wavering inflexions of five or six 'Ariel' poems. But mainly, if there is not silence or near silence (with so much now known-through and not worth the saying), or the grand harmonizing of all inflexions (bespeaking all the errors of experience against original impulses towards a good desire) as in *King Lear*, there is a peculiarly large tumult—expressed through the voice—of all grammatical Tenses and Moods. For in this period, a poet either ceases to write (through a sense of sheer inadequacy of his technique to project what he has to say), or he now writes his greatest work.

[1] T. S. Eliot, *Burnt Norton*.

PART TWO

PARTICULAR
VOICES

IV The Voice of Tennyson

To what extent are the special qualities of Tennyson's poetry the result of the properties of his physical voice? The content of the speech, and even the writing, in so far as this is orally conceived, of all persons is, as we have suggested, conditioned to some extent by the voice of the speaker or writer. A meaning is modified by its envelope of sound; conversely, a voice chooses what it can best communicate. But if this is the case with all people it is more particularly true of poets, those whose function it is to transmit organized patterns of sound. Or, to put the question negatively: Was Tennyson, as a poet, confined within the limits of his personal voice? I shall suggest that he was such a prisoner. Sometimes indeed he attempted to break out and to write in a voice other than his own, to write, that is, lines which he could not effectively recite aloud; but then the effect seems false, possibly disastrous. It seems on these occasions that Tennyson is writing of things he had never experienced nor could experience, things which he neither had nor could convincingly vocalize. For Tennyson was, as critics agree, almost entirely a lyrical poet, one who wrote of his own feelings in his own person. Even at his most descriptive, in, say, the narrative mould of the *Idylls*, the description is bound to a lyrical impulse. Lyrical poets are specifically 'I' poets, poets who utter—explicitly or implicitly—in the First Person Singular, in their own persons, that is, in their own physical voices. But Tennyson's own voice is heard as strongly in narrative as in lyric. Only when it is not heard, when he is trying to speak like someone else, does the result naturally sound grotesque or unconvincing. In the main however, Tennyson was a willing prisoner of his voice, for it

47

was a large and magnificent prison. What did it sound like to others and to himself?

In the second volume of the *Poems*, published in 1842, there is a piece called 'The Epic'. It serves as a prologue or induction to 'Morte d'Arthur' which, with alteration and additions, was to be republished under the title of 'The Passing of Arthur' in 1869.[1] Now 'The Epic' is written in the easy, even-toned, middle-pitched conversational voice that Tennyson assumes when he wants to be thought of as relaxed and genial. But it is a deceptively easy tone because it is one Tennyson adopts—as a preparation and as a precaution—when what he really intends is the saying or confession of something that stirs the roots of his being. The same method, or lead up to intimacy, is followed in *The Princess*. There his confessional lamentations, those near-tremulous and profoundly felt poems, such as

> Tears, idle tears, I know not what they mean . . .

or

> Now sleeps the crimson petal, now the white . . .

or

> The splendour falls on castle walls . . .

which we recognize as the essential Tennyson, are protectively introduced, and followed, by an easy blank verse. Its easiness is deceptive. We know in actual life how the studiously casual remark is a self-protective method of introduction adopted by one person towards another when he has news of great emotional importance to impart, and is either unsure of the response or wants to condition the response. This method of manner and tone Tennyson adopts, in the person of Everard Hall in 'The Epic', to erect for himself a guard by deceiving others into thinking that what is to follow is not a *cri de coeur*, when indeed it is. By this means he hopes to avert a too closely pressed enquiry about something so personal: for what is to follow this casual introduction is nothing less than an allegory of the death of Arthur Hallam. In the terms of this allegory

---

[1] It was deeply characteristic of Tennyson that he should have written the last of the *Idylls* first—that the 'Morte' or 'Passing' was the foreordained conclusion of the whole series. In the morning of his life he was brooding on evening farewells.

'Morte d'Arthur' confessed the gravest and most grievous event
in the whole of Tennyson's experience.   Therefore 'The Epic'
begins casually:

> At Francis Allen's on the Christmas-eve—
> The game of forfeits done—the girls all kiss'd
> Beneath the sacred bush and past away—
> The parson Holmes, the poet Everard Hall,
> The host, and I sat round the wassail-bowl . . . .

Then Everard Hall, or Tennyson—for only the smaller part
of Tennyson is that 'I', an auditor, though he would 'distance'
'Morte d'Arthur' by pretending it the work of another—is
persuaded to read the eleventh, and only surviving, book of the
epic he had composed in his Cambridge undergraduate days:

> and the poet little urged,
> But with some prelude of disparagement,
> Read, mouthing out his hollow oes and aes,
> Deep-chested music, and to this result . . . .

To what result? To the result we know so well from our hearing
when Tennyson, deeply moved, is speaking in his own voice:

> So all day long the noise of battle roll'd
> Among the mountains by the winter sea
> Until King Arthur's table, man by man,
> Had fall'n in Lyonesse about their Lord,
> King Arthur: then, because his wound was deep,
> The bold Sir Bedivere uplifted him,
> Sir Bedivere, the last of all his knights,
> And bore him to a chapel nigh the field,
> A broken chancel with a broken cross,
> That stood on a dark strait of barren land.
> On one side lay the Ocean, and on one
> Lay a great water, and the moon was full.

That Everard Hall's manner of saying Tennyson's poetry
was Tennyson's we have evidence. In 1855, at the house of
D. G. Rossetti, there was a gathering at which Tennyson and
Browning read aloud their poems. Tennyson read *Maud*. W. M.
Rossetti, who was present, reported on the contrasting voices
of the two poets: whereas Browning is described as reading in a

high-pitched jerky voice, emphasizing all the dramatic shades of his verse, Tennyson is described as 'mouthing out his hollow oes and aes'.

'Mouthing out his hollow oes and aes'. W. M. Rossetti in 1855 is certainly remembering the Everard Hall of 1842 and his 'deep-chested music'. And others remembered Tennyson's self-description and compared it with their own. Thus Edward Fitzgerald:

> Mouthing out his hollow oes and aes, deep-chested music, this is something as A. T. reads, with a broad north country vowel, except the u in such words as 'much', 'brute', which he pronounces like the thin French 'u'. His voice, very deep and deep-chested, but rather murmuring than mouthing, like the sound of a far sea or of a pine-wood, I remember greatly struck Carlyle when he first came to know him. . . . Sometimes Spedding would read the poems to us; A. T. once told him he seemed to read too much as if bees were about his mouth.[1]

Now we might ask whether by 1855 the 'deep-chested music' of 1842 had become yet deeper. But delaying an answer to that question, let us consider the '*hollow* oes and aes', of which Tennyson—as Hall—was conscious, and perhaps consciously exploited. By 'hollow' oes he probably means long, and not short, oes, the kind of 'o' in both syllables of 'hollow' and not the 'o' in 'not'. He probably means those oes which, provided they were uttered in the right (i.e. pleasing to Tennyson) acoustic conditions—viz. in a room (and with an audience) small enough to make a high, or even middle pitch, and a loud volume, unnecessary for audibility, and yet a *reverberative* room. Such conditions permit a deep and slow delivery. As we know both from *Tennyson: a memoir* and from *Tennyson and his Friends*, Tennyson was never so happy or so fully himself as when reading his own poems, new or old, aloud to his friends. Whenever there were visitors, which was often, either at Faringford or Aldworth, this is how they were entertained after dinner: a small but appreciative audience in a reverberative room gathered to hear the poet read aloud. And all those who heard, and who reported their experience, agree—so far as subjective qualitative descriptions can agree—as to the kind of voice Tennyson's was

[1] *Tennyson: a memoir* by Hallam Tennyson, second edition, London 1899, p. 162.

and as to the manner it was exercised. Listeners were 'spell-bound'.[1] Afterwards, and in a cooler mood, it was possible to be somewhat critical. Thus Palgrave:

> None of his friends, and few even among occasional visitors, failed to hear him read. What poetical recitation, as distinguished alike from mere reading and from dramatic utterance, should be, no definite theory seems to exist; no authoritative code. Tastes at any rate here differ widely; and casual hearers have found Tennyson's method too little varied or emphatic, his voice and delivery monotonous. Yet those who knew the speaker could easily see causes which explained and justified his method. Tennyson's grand range and 'timbre' of voice; his power of modulation; his great *sostenuto* power; the *portamento* so justly dear to Italian vocalists, might be the truer word; the ample resonant utterance: all was simply no deliberate art of recital but the direct outward representative, the effluence at once of his own deepest sentiment as to what Poetry should be, and of the intention, the aspiration of his own poems.

[1] See Margaret L. Wood: 'The Great Voice of Victorian England' in *Tennyson and his Friends*, p. 185. The phrase was less worn than it is now. The listeners included Edmund Lushington: 'the deep melodious thunder of his [Tennyson's] voice, with all its overwhelming pathos', *Memoir*, p. 169. Sir Henry Taylor: 'Something in the lofty brow and acquiline nose suggests Dante, but such a deep mellow chest-voice never could have come from Italian lungs', *Ibid.*, p. 353. Miss Emily Ritchie: 'Nothing was more memorable than to hear him read his poetry. The roll of his great voice acted sometimes almost like an incantation, so that when it was a new poem he was reading, the power of realizing its actual nature was subordinated to the wonder at the sound of the tones. Sometimes, as in "The Passing of Arthur", it was a long chant, in which the expression lay chiefly in the value given to each syllable, sometimes a swell of sound like an organ's; often came tones of infinite pathos, delicate and tender, then others of mighty volume and passionate strength', *Ibid.*, p. 76. F. T. Palgrave: 'Many who heard them so spoken [i.e. Tennyson's sounding of his own poems] will agree, these can never be heard again, no, nor read, to similar advantage. Something of their music, some part of their very essence, has passed with the Maker', *Ibid.*, p. 835. Sir James Knowles: 'It was not reading as usually understood, but intoning on a note, almost chanting, which I heard, and which brought the conviction that this was the proper vehicle for poetry as distinguished from prose', *Tennyson and his Friends*, p. 247. The most detailed account of his performance of a particular poem ('De Profundis') is by Wilfred Ward, and is to be found in Appendix A (p. 475) of *Tennyson and his Friends*. The poems which, up to the end of his life, he most enjoyed performing were, according to his son (*Memoir*, p. 324), 'Maud', 'The Ode to the Duke of Wellington' and 'Guinevere'.

The criticism Palgrave implies of the manner of delivery is as much a criticism of the poetry itself, and the defence he brings to the delivery is a defence of the poetry, for the two are one. Hence he continues:

> Such had they sung themselves to him, as he thought them out, often keeping them, even when of considerable length, in memory before a syllable was placed on paper: and in strict accordance with that inner music was the audible rendering of it. Whether this conformed to common practice or not, 'he could no otherwise'.[1]

'Deep-chested music': if the music is to be 'deep-chested' it must be sounded slowly if the meaning is not to be smothered by the resonance or by outer reverberation. Therefore, Tennyson, it might seem, composed for his instrument; he wrote lines that he could effectively sound aloud—lines such as

> The long day wanes: the slow moon climbs: the deep
> Moans round with many voices. . . .

These lines from *Ulysses*, published 1842, are but one illustration of Tennyson's 'oes', and an 'o' is one letter which stands not for one but for a variety of related sounds and for a variety of phonemes of each of those sounds. But the long and hollow oes are enormously frequent in Tennyson's poetry and, together with the open and long aes, do indeed create or constitute its dominant tonal (or sonal) character.

I do not know the acoustics of that small top room at Aldworth, where the composing and recitation both mainly took place, except by inference. But that the oes in 'long', 'slow', 'moon', 'moans' (though this is from a poem before the Aldworth period) were apprehended by Tennyson as long and hollow to match, and chiefly convey, his mood there can be little doubt. Admittedly 'long', 'slow', 'moon', 'moans' *can* be said lightly and snappily out of context, and if the speaker is perverse in intention, but to reduce the quantity of sounds naturally long, and to do so in a context where that natural length is increased by mood and meaning is to be more than perverse—deaf. As the sea sounded to Tennyson, given his

---

[1] *Memoir*, pp. 834–835.

melancholy temperament, so he would make it sound; he had the voice to do it.

'Immeasurable sadness' has ever required a deep (in pitch) and slow (in tempo) utterance. Moreover the punctuation, strictly regarded, of the quoted lines further emphasizes the manner in which Tennyson apprehended and spoke them. If he was, as a poet, the prisoner of his voice, then his voice was made for grief. Hallam's death confirmed the disposition of his temperament and encouraged him to indulge his vocal strength and particularity.

Not, of course, that the sounding of 'hollow oes and aes' (the two vowel sounds which can in fact be most easily prolonged in English without appearing unnatural) represent the limit of Tennyson's virtuosity as an exploiter of vocal sounds. That would be an absurd proposition. But the 'hollow oes and aes' are his gravitational centre. Like any other poet he employs every sound in the vowel scale, but it is from the 'hollow oes and aes' that he departs and to which he returns. These are his auditory correlatives of brooding sadness. A frequent departure from the dominant brooding sadness was towards a wild hopeless anguish and then his voice rose in the employment of vowels high, desolate but thrilling. Somewhat harsh too, for we remember that Carlyle said his voice was not only musical but also 'metallic'. He also said that Tennyson's voice was fit 'for piercing wail'.

The obvious place to hear that is in *The Idylls*. The following passage, for instance, begins and ends with a series of sounds in which the Tennysonian 'hollow oes and aes', deep-chested, slowly-uttered, resonant, are dominant. But from this rumbling ground-bass the 'piercing wail' rises. Tennyson is probably exploiting the resources of his own voice, composing—or sounding—his poetry to the full extent of his voice's limits, but notice how successfully his own 'piercing wail' coincides with the objective meaning of the lines: for it is the wail of the three Queens which the narrator vocally echoes. We have just been told that the barge, which has 'hove' in sight, is crowded with stately forms

> Black-stoled, black-hooded, like a dream—by these
> Three Queens with crowns of gold—and from them rose
> A cry that shiver'd to the tingling stars,

And, as it were one voice, an agony
Of lamentation, like a wind that shrills
All night in a waste land, where no one comes
Or hath come, since the making of the world.

To compliment Tennyson on a successful piece of onoma-
topoeia is unnecessary after listening to one of the most thrilling
'effects' in all poetry. The point is, rather, that we have been
listening—and listening to Tennyson's voice.[1] If the poet had
been unable to conceive of his own voice creating such an effect
it is doubtful whether the words would now exist in print.
Moreover it is interesting that although the quoted passage
appeared in Volume II of *Poems 1842*, another passage, equally
remarkable as a demonstration of Tennyson's ability to voice a
piercing wail, had to wait till 1869 when it appeared as an
addition to the 1842 *Morte d'Arthur*. It was one of those additions
which helped to shift the tendency of the poem from a concentration on a death—the death of Hallam and Arthur of
Britain—to a concentration on a less final 'passing' (such a
Victorian, such a comforting, word—later to become 'passing
on' or 'over'!) leaving a reunion open, or possible, or likely.
Perhaps that death of 1835 had become no longer bearable to
contemplate as an extinction. Certainly, between 1842 and 1869,
In Memoriam had been conceived and written, and in that poem,
if only as a speculation (and, to the dread of Tennyson perhaps,
only as a *speculation* it remained), Arthur had transcended his
death:

Thy voice is on the rolling air;
I hear thee where the waters run;
Thou standest in the rising sun,
And in the setting thou art fair.[2]

That the 1869 'Passing of Arthur' included more of the 'piercing wail' may be partly attributed to the change in Tennyson's

[1] In an early review of *Idylls of the King*, reprinted in *The Wind and the Rain
Yearbook*, 1961, and attributed there (by Norman St John Stevas) to Walter
Bagehot, the writer makes some revealing comments on Tennyson's reliance
on soliloquies and avoidance of dialogue and 'the remarkable similarity
of the conversational powers of all the various personages'. It is as though
Tennyson, in lending his own voice to all the personages, was obliged to
make all of them profess matter suitable to that voice.

[2] *In Memoriam*, CXXIX.

feelings towards Hallam and partly to his discovery that his voice could make the piercing wail with such surpassing effect. Thus:

> Then, ere that last weird battle in the west,
> There came on Arthur sleeping, Gawain kill'd
> In Lancelot's war, the ghost of Gawain blown
> Along a wandering wind, and past his ear
> Went shrilling, 'Hollow, hollow all delight!
> Hail, King! to-morrow thou shalt pass away.
> Farewell! there is an isle of rest for thee.
> And I am blown along a wandering wind,
> And hollow, hollow, hollow all delight.'
> And fainter onward, like wild birds that change
> Their season in the night and wail their way
> From cloud to cloud, down the long wind the dream
> Shrill'd; but in going mingled with the dim cries
> Far in the moonlit haze among the hills,
> As of some lonely city sack'd by night,
> When all is lost, and wife and child with wail
> Pass to new lords; and Arthur woke and call'd,
> 'Who spoke? A dream. O light upon the wind,
> Thine, Gawain, was the voice—are these dim cries
> Thine? or doth all that haunts the waste and wild
> Mourn, knowing it will go along with me?'

Tennyson since 1842 had found out what his voice could do in the way of this departure from his vocal norm or gravitational centre and is here composing as if for performance by himself. And that he did compose for his own voice, and with it, we have the evidence of his son, Hallam:

It was then that my father worked at 'Maud', morning and evening, sitting in his hard high-backed wooden chair in his little room at the top of the house. His 'sacred pipes', as he called them, were half an hour after breakfast, and half an hour after dinner [This dinner period was later extended.] when no one was allowed to be with him, for then his best thoughts came to him. As he made the different poems he would repeat or read them. The constant reading of the new poems aloud was the surest way of helping him to find out any defects there might be. During his 'sacred half-hours' and his other working hours and even on the Downs, he would murmur his new passages or new lines as they came to him,

E 55

a habit which had always been his since boyhood, and which caused the Somersby cook to say 'What is master Alfred always a praying for?'[1]

Though he composed 'The Passing of Arthur', no less than his other work, to the sound of his own voice, Tennyson was right in terming it an Idyll rather than a part of an epic. The quoted lines, as much as those that are 'deep-chested', from which they rise as a variant, can only be properly, that is effectively, realized in a smallish room occupied by few auditors. They would sound wan, thin and weak in an auditorium on the scale conceived by Milton. They depended for their effect ('effect' need not be taken as critically pejorative) precisely on their being a variant from the habitual 'deep-chested' resonantal music from which they rise startlingly upward. But such 'deep-chested music' required a small echoic room, and therefore a limited audience. It could not be generated in the Albert Hall nor even, as anyone who has had experience of the microphone will realize, from a BBC studio. In the broadcasting studio, and the engineers would seem to have their reasons, extremes of pitch are rendered impossible.

I suggested that the insertion of the passage just quoted into the 1869 version is also to be related to Tennyson's changed feelings towards the dead Hallam: it represents perhaps an accomplished absorption of that great blow which was likewise the main event of his life. An 'accomplished absorption' is something more than resignation. It may be that a very long brooded-on grief—grief, an emotion which in any poem or any situation of actual life expresses itself in low or sunken tones—is driven sometimes to seek relief in a scream, but in Tennyson's case the absorption or resignation probably brought a state of detachment in which such a scream of relief could be employed as a conscious artistic effect. Safely employed, because in the *Idylls* he is ostensibly being a narrative and not a lyrical or

---

[1] *Memoir*, pp. 317–318. So we turn up that Somersby cook and we find that her wonder was shared by other folk in that area who thought the poet 'crazed'. A fisherman, for instance, was puzzled. When the young Tennyson met this fisherman at 4 a.m. and bade him Good morning, the fisherman replied, 'Thou poor fool, thou doesn't knaw whether it be night or daä.' *Tennyson and his Friends*, p. 15.

confessional poet. As a narrative poet, engaged on a national theme, he could let out the relieving scream of desolation which his reticence, his sense of shame, would have forbidden in a poem written in the first person.

But the 'piercing wail' is, as we have said, a departure: it is the 'hollow oes and aes' that are most essentially Tennysonian. To these we return in such lines as:

> The woods decay, the woods decay and fall,
> The vapours weep their burthen to the ground,
> Man comes and tills the field and lies beneath,
> And after many a summer dies the swan.[1]

And a question to be asked is: If this is Tennyson's central poetic voice in 1860 (not necessarily his customary talking voice—for that refer to the early 'Epic' or the late 'Lines to E. Fitzgerald'), in what way had it changed, if at all, from his earlier—1842—poetic voice, the voice with which he composed, say, 'The Lady of Shalott' or 'The Dying Swan'?

Now Tennyson's 'falling rhythms' have been remarked on by G. Wilson Knight. I shall here extend the term to include not only the poet's metrical or rhythmical propensities (e.g. the feminine endings of 'The Lady of Shalott' or 'The Lotus Eaters') but also his specifically vocal pattern, and shall try to show that both rhythm and voice agree with the meaning of the poetry. The opening lines of *Tithonus* provide a key example. What the lines say is 'that trees fall, that the rain falls ("The vapours weep their burthen to the ground"), that Man falls and lies below the fields he once tilled, and that even the long-lived swan also eventually succumbs'. The four lines state four parallel instances of declension. The instances of mortality are literal instances of 'falling' for, when we dedicate a war memorial 'To the Fallen', 'fallen' is at least as literal as metaphorical. But the extremely characteristic meaning of the lines is at one with their sound or—more exactly—with the contours of Tennyson's voice. Whether the morbidly melancholy temperament has governed the down-curves of the voice, or whether the qualities of the voice—the effects it could, on the basis of

---

[1] Opening of 'Tithonus', first published in 1860.

experience, most triumphantly achieve—has chiefly conditioned the mood of the lines (the mood of most of his lines, of most of his poems) we cannot absolutely determine.

Yet 'as a man speaks so he is', and the four lines, whose meaning is decline, must in Tennyson's voice, or in ours when we hear that voice and repeat the lines, trace four lines as on a graph, each of which ends with a falling movement or droop. Each line ends with lowered pitch, that is the vowels or diphthongs in 'fall' [ɔɪ], 'ground' [au], '-neath' [iː] and 'swan' [ɔ] are the lowest of the series of each line, in which they respectively occur. I am aware of the argument that any voice can say any vowel at whatever pitch (and can give it any length) the owner pleases and is within his capacity. But this argument, in practice if not theory, is nonsense. There is a vowel scale, and in this scale the natural pitch of i in 'hit' is higher (and shorter) than the natural pitch of aɪ in 'father'. If this is true of individual sounds, it is truer still of sounds in the order of natural speech where the semantics of the context of the individual sounds fortifies their natural pitch; but it is truest of all in poetry generally, but especially so in the case of a poet who, like Tennyson, exploited the vowel scale, in terms of his own vocal instrument, to the extent of accentuating or emphasizing natural pitch and natural quantity. I am also aware that ɔ as in 'swan' is only an approximate and, because an approximate, inaccurate sign. The vowel alters pitch and tonal colour when it is restored to the word from which it is abstracted. Then the consonants modify the vowel they precede or follow. It is a fact that ɔ when it is followed by the voiced nasal n, as in 'swan', is lower in pitch and longer than ɔ in 'not'. And when we move from the final vowel of each line, whether separately considered in the natural scale or as modified by preceding or succeeding consonant, to the line as a whole, then we see that the semantics and the phonology are married. We perceive that each line ends with a veritable vowel fall. Anything but bracing poetry!—but essential Tennyson, something which his voice, interacting with temperament, conditioned him to say aloud while writing. We notice that in each line there is a pitch summit, from which decline follows, and we also notice the long medial and line-terminal pauses—pauses required for the absorption of resonance which has been generated by a series of vowel-sounds which have been chosen for their long duration.[1] Certainly, by contrast, the word 'tills' is short enough and its vowel short and high in the vowel scale. But that is appropriate. 'Man comes', and he is above the field and Tennyson's voice rises on that 'tills'. But he is above for only a short while, and the weighted pauses after 'comes' and after 'field' bracket and point that brief rising arc of sound. The pitch returns to the norm with the 'and lies beneath'.

How does the voice of the mature Tennyson, using the person of Tithonus,[2] compare with the voice of the younger Tennyson using the person of The Lady of Shalott? How did the voice of the younger Tennyson contain the voice of a woman—and the earlier poems are full of complaints or lamentations by bereaved or jilted women, of Madeleines, Marianas, Isabellas, etc.? Here he is not speaking *through* the Lady of Shalott, but nevertheless he is speaking very much *with* her. The sorrowful landscape reflects the Lady's mood and is the correct pictorial setting for her action:

> In the stormy east-wind straining,
> The pale yellow woods were waning,
> The broad stream in his banks complaining,
> Heavily the low sky raining
>> Over tower'd Camelot;
> Down she came and found a boat
> Beneath a willow left afloat,
> And round about the prow she wrote
>> *The Lady of Shalott*.

> And down the river's dim expanse—
> Like some bold seer in a trance,
> Seeing all his own mischance—
> With a glassy countenance
>> Did she look to Camelot.

[1] Their natural length has been extended by the emotion and meaning of the words, and the phrases, in which they occur; also by the choice of consonant following the vowel. Example: in 'The vapours weep their burthen to the ground' the u [əi] of 'burthen' has been lengthened by the following 'th'—by Tennyson's choice of the variant 'burthen' instead of 'burden'.

[2] I am aware that *Tithonus* was composed 'even upward of a quarter of a century' before its appearance in *The Cornhill*. Tennyson, in a letter to the Duke of Argyll in 1860, said that 'it was originally a pendant to *Ulysses*'.

And at the closing of the day
She loosed the chain, and down she lay;
The broad stream bore her far away,
    The Lady of Shalott.

Compared with the voice in Tithonus the voice *with* the
Lady of Shalott is lighter. It is the same voice but at two
different stages of life. The trochaics of 'The Lady' naturally
create a 'falling rhythm', but the iambics of 'Tithonus' also
create a 'falling rhythm', perhaps even more pronounced. But
Tennyson in the earlier poem is lamenting or complaining in
a voice—his own—which yet contains a woman's, even a
maiden's. Tennyson's wonderful organ, for all its 'deep-
chestedness', its murmuringness, its sonority (but without
the edge of harshness, such as we hear in Milton whenever he
approaches to anger which is frequent) *included* a voice of
female timbre and range, capable both of expressing the
'piercing wail' of the three Queens (in *The Passing of Arthur*)
and the more subdued complaints of young women or
maidens who have been deserted, such as Claribel, Lilian,
Isabel, Mariana, Madeleine or Adeline. But, as the com-
prehensive voice of the man Tennyson deepened with age, so
did the woman's voice it included, and the voices of Oenone,
Eleanore and, in the *Idylls*, of Enid, Elaine and Guinevere
are lower and less girlish than those of the earlier heroines.
And we have only to reflect on this included female voice to
understand a little more that strange work, *The Princess*. Into
that 'Medley' of women's voices, of men's while masquerading
as women, and of women's aspirations, he smuggled most of
the heart-felt lyrics he ever wrote, including 'Now sleeps the
crimson petal, now the white', 'The splendour falls on castle
walls' and 'Tears, idle tears, I know not what they mean'.[1]
(And let us take a stand on this at once, and say that Tennyson's incapacity—however he tried, in *Locksley Hall* and elsewhere—to give his voice the sharp or harsh edge of cruel or
vindictive anger of a hard man was to his honour. It is to our
own loss when we mistake, as we often mistake, gentleness for
softness.)

---

[1] The qualification 'most' is needed because of such lyrics as 'Break,
break, break' and 'Crossing the Bar'.

Hence the inclusion of the woman's voice explains the pitch-graph or contour of

> In the stormy east-wind straining,
> The pale yellow woods were waning,
> The broad stream in his banks complaining,
> Heavily the low sky raining . . .

where the penultimate syllable in each line rises high in the scale of grief only to drop, hopelessly and nervelessly, in the last. For it is true that women, when bewailing a grief, trace a vocal contour of this kind, rising with each phrase to a wail followed immediately by a drop, while men's voices, in such a situation, maintain a leaded hollowness, as indeed we have heard in *Tithonus*. Each sex, in the state of sorrow, accentuates its vocal differential.

Now, of course, the imagery of *The Lady of Shalott* is as much at one with its vocal contours (I use 'contour' so as to avoid the encumbering ambiguity of 'melodic line') as the imagery of the opening of *Tithonus* is at one with *its* vocal contours. In both poems the landscape is sympathetically autumnal and leaves are falling:

> The woods decay, the woods decay and fall . . . (*Tithonus*)
> The pale yellow woods were waning . . . (*The Lady of Shalott*)

but, though both lines trace a falling rhythm, the pitch-values of the second line quoted are, according to the natural scale, higher. Because the vowels of 'pale', and the accentuated vowels of 'yellow' and 'waning' are higher than in the line from *Tithonus* they are consequently shorter and, because shorter, do not require following pauses of the same weight for the absorption of resonance. Nevertheless, like *Tithonus*, each line ends with a fall in sound and meaning, and the whole poem conveys a decline or descent. The Lady floats in her craft down the river (the very word 'down' appears three times in the stanzas quoted), and all else is flagging or falling.

A comparison of *The Lady of Shalott* and *Tithonus* has shown that the voice of Tennyson hardly changed, only deepened. Not that it needed to change since he did not alter his theme, or substance, but simply devoted more resources for expressing that theme. That theme expresses a stupendous loss, whether confessed in the first person as in *In Memoriam* or vicariously through the persons of others, especially women, and that loss induces him to ponder his own days and years, since that loss, as posthumous, as a 'death in life':

O Death in Life, the days that are no more.

It is no wonder, then, that his most central, or deepest, voice was reserved for the expression of grief (a backward-looking emotion as joy is a forward-looking emotion), or, alternatively, it is no wonder that he chose this theme for his chief one since he had a physical voice that could express 'immeasurable sadness' so well.[1] The poems of grief, consequent upon desertion or bereavement, are in Tennyson's deepest or most central voice. The deepest voice is, in Tennyson, the most central. That recognized, we are open to admit that Tennyson had other voices—off-centre or marginal ones. Tennyson, as we all do, acted, and could act, like all of us, sincerely. Each of us has his or her central voice, the one we reserve for the communication of that which touches us most nearly, but all of us 'put on' voices appropriate to the repertoire of masks we don for many occasions. This or that occasion, we consider, demands this or that kind of voice. Depending on our interlocutors, depending on the situation, so we (excepting those situations when we have, or wish to, expose or disclose our very selves) 'assume' a voice. Now Tennyson was perhaps obliged to assume a voice, that was not his central voice, whenever he wrote outside his chosen, or fated, theme. Examples of these marginal voices are the cosy, nearly infantile voice, that we hear in his contributions to various albums and annuals, the martial and patriotic voice that he assumed for the celebration of national occasions.

Sometimes we recognize our own false notes (though we hope others do not) when we 'put on' a voice too remote from our central one. Yet our adopted voices, Tennyson's no less, have this peculiarity: only the speaker can adopt them, and sound

[1] I am aware that Tennyson wrote poems of bereavement *before* Hallam died. This does not necessarily oblige one to choose the alternative explanation. Even while Hallam was living, Tennyson probably dreaded his death, dreaded being left alone.

just so. As an example of a Tennyson 'put-on' voice here is an
arch, saucy gentlewoman speaking in the 'Shakespearean'
Becket:

> Babble in bower
>   Under the rose!
> Bee mustn't buzz,
>   Whoop—but he knows.
>
> Kiss me, little one,
>   Nobody near!
> Grasshopper, grasshopper,
>   Whoop—you can hear.
>
> Kiss in the bower,
>   Tit on the tree!
> Bird mustn't tell,
>   Whoop—he can see.

As for the martial Tennyson—well, we all know the *Charge
of the Light Brigade*, wherein he used a voice which could
almost convince himself. This poem is the 'text' of the gramophone recording he made two years before his death. Despite
the imperfections of technique in recording at that date, and
despite the background noises, we can hear the poet's voice,
tremulous with age, enacting a bravado it could not feel. What
he does not need to enact is the essential melancholy that indulges itself in selecting a *failure*, a military loss—though a
public or impersonal one—to celebrate.

More interesting than these marginal voices is, probably, the
voice of the poems in Lincolnshire dialect. This group of poems
forms a distinctive group in the work of Tennyson. For one
thing they are genuinely narrative poems and so have characters and a story. The characters—I think especially of the
Northern Farmer—are spry, humorous, hard-hearted, hard-
fisted, cunning and mean. Their language, because it *is* a dialect, is peculiar to such characters; it can hardly be adequately
represented by the simple use of diacritics and a modification
of standard English orthography, and it can hardly be spoken
by any but a native of Lincolnshire. The speakers of this dialect
express their local history and experience. It reflects that history
and experience; it also reflects the speakers' ethnic variation,

another peculiarity. Tennyson could lapse into his native dialect—or return to it—by an act of memory, or by purposefully forgetting or jettisoning all those characteristics he had acquired either as a suffering individual or as a public figure and 'bard'. When an 'educated' individual returns to his dialect it implies a shedding of his individuality in order to return to a primitive group.

With the exception of those in dialect, Tennyson's poetry is anything—either in sound or meaning, though the sound in Tennyson is almost a substitute for meaning—but 'spry, humorous, hard-hearted, hard-fisted, cunning and mean'. He represents the opposite of such qualities: but the opposite may have resulted from an instinctive, or at any rate only half-understood, reaction—a reaction against the family and tribe (a reaction that all individuals must undertake in order to arrive at being individual; a reaction whereby an individual gains his own new voice only at the expense of murdering—or 'living down' or suppressing—the old). Nevertheless, at some time the individual may feel a nostalgic caprice to imitate the old.

However that might be, it is certain that in his dialect poems the language fits the characters and their mean thoughts and crafty actions. Tennyson, in these poems, perhaps consciously 'lapsed', or humorously condescended. Whatever his motive (and it is as difficult to attribute 'motive' to great poets as it is to criminals in the dock), Tennyson, in his dialect poems, released aspects of his personality which otherwise would have remained buried and silent. And the curious thing is that the public liked his 'Northern Farmer' poems (as Mr Eliot's public liked his 'Practical Cats') when they were published in 1846, and this liking induced him to try his hand again. Again with humorous condescension? But the public, beyond liking genuine tragi-comic, yet universal, situations, probably liked this giving away of himself by Mr Tennyson ('Come down, O maid, from yonder height . . .'), and egged him on. Admitted to a privacy within a privacy, they were delighted with, and curious about, a voice that lay beneath the bardic roll or desperate wail.

That Tennyson was haunted by sound generally and particularly within the bounds of his own voice, and that he composed in terms of his own voice, is the argument here. He was a prisoner of that voice, however capacious the dimensions of that prison. I am not aiming to be clever at the expense of a great voice, and a simple and great and a nervous man whom we all ought to devoutly admire, but it is inevitable that we should conclude with two quotations which have probably been used, but less sympathetically, against this poet before.

The first is this: 'Before I could read, I was in the habit on a stormy day of spreading my arms to the wind, and crying out "I hear a voice that's crying in the wind" '.[1] These are the first words, and the first line, that anyone remembers Tennyson to have 'echoed'. And the other, from *In Memoriam*:

> But what am I?
> An infant crying in the night,
> An infant crying for the light,
> And with no language but a cry.

Yet the timbre and vocal projection of that cry (literally understood) was unique and will never be heard exactly again unless we recover the voice behind the printed signs on the page.

[1] Tennyson in 1890, *Memoir*, p. 9.

V The Voice of Shelley

T HAT the work of some poets is expressed by, that it can be
controlled, or conditioned, or—negatively—limited by, the
properties of their physical voices is a proposition that finds
admirable support in the case of Shelley. The voice that we
hear with the 'inner ear' when reading the poetry of Shelley—
that is if we read poetry as we ought to, receiving the voice of
the poet through or behind the printed signs—is high-pitched
and rapid. The voice of the poet, on the evidence of one who
suffered from it a good deal, agrees with the voice of the poetry.

In 1832, ten years after Shelley's death, Thomas Jefferson
Hogg published a series of reminiscences of his friend, later col-
lected under the title *Shelley at Oxford*. Hogg and Shelley were
fellow undergraduates at University College, Oxford, and they
were both sent down after the latter's publication of *The
Necessity of Atheism*. Of course Hogg's memoirs of his friend are
well-known, but I am concerned here with those passages
that mention Shelley's voice. Shelley's voice was precisely what
struck Hogg most. I aim to relate the significance of what bulks
so prominently in Hogg's *Shelley at Oxford* to Shelley's poetry.[1]

This is how Hogg recalls his impressions after Shelley had
eventually departed after his first visit:

> I admired the enthusiasm of my new acquaintance, his ardour
> in the cause of science and his thirst for knowledge. I seemed to
> have found in him all those intellectual qualities which I had

[1] References are to *Shelley at Oxford* with an introduction by R. A. Streat-
field, London, 1904.

vainly expected to meet with in a University. But there was one physical blemish that threatened to neutralise all his excellence. 'This is a fine, clever fellow!' I said to myself, 'but I can never bear his society; I shall never be able to bear his voice; it would kill me. What a pity it is!' I am very sensible of imperfections, and especially of painful sounds, and the voice of the stranger was excruciating. It was intolerably shrill, harsh and discordant; of the most cruel intension. It was perpetual, and without any remission; it excoriated my ears.[1]

Shelley had left Hogg's rooms in order to attend a lecture on chemistry and Hogg had debated whether to ask him back to tea after the lecture: 'I am ashamed to own that the cruel voice made me hesitate for a moment; but it was impossible to omit so indispensable a civility—I invited him to return to tea.'[2] Shelley in fact returned to tea and stayed on to supper, and then held forth as avidly as ever: 'He discoursed after supper with as much warmth as before of the wonders of chemistry. . . . The voice, however, seemed to me more cruel than ever.'[3]

Despite that voice and, as is known, one can get accustomed to most things, the friendship between Shelley and Hogg flourished during that session at great intensity. They met to talk, though it would seem that Shelley did most of the talking, Hogg most of the listening. Though they shared interests, they had also complementary temperaments which favoured friendship. Hogg's part in the friendship was that of listener and irritant. He would draw out Shelley and set the rapturous voice going and, when it lapsed, would revive it with his occasional down-to-earth objections. Nevertheless Shelley was silent when he was asleep, though it was a sleep that refreshed his vocal energy. Hogg gives us a delightful, because vivid and affectionate, *vignette*:

At six he would suddenly compose himself, even in the midst of a most animated narrative or of earnest discussion; and he would lie buried in entire forgetfulness, in a sweet and mighty oblivion, until ten, when he would suddenly start up, and rubbing his eyes with great violence, and passing his fingers swiftly through his long hair, would enter at once into a vehement argument, or begin to recite verses, either of his own composition or from the

---

[1] P. 12, *op. cit.*   [2] P. 13, *ibid.*   [3] P. 16, *ibid.*

works of others, with a rapidity and an energy that were often quite painful.[1]

Shelley's voice is likened to the voice of a peacock:

> I was maintaining against him one day at my rooms the superiority of the ethical sciences over the physical. In the course of the debate he cried with shrill vehemence—for as his aspect presented to the eye much of the elegance of the peacock, he cruelly lacerated the ear with its discordant tones—'You talk of the preeminence of moral philosophy? Do you comprehend politics under that name?'[2]

Here are extended examples from Hogg's reminiscences. But throughout the book there are *en passant* references to Shelley's voice. Thus, for example, Hogg, after the first meeting, pays a return call on Shelley. He finds the direction from description; he taps at the door and realizes he has come to the right place when 'the discordant voice cried shrilly, "Come in!" ' Or Shelley expresses an enthusiastic scorn: ' "What faces! What an expression of countenance! What wretched beings!" Here he clasped his hands and raised his voice to a painful pitch, with fervid dislike.'[3]

That Hogg, sensitive as he says to 'painful sounds', presented a faithful description of Shelley's personality (and therefore of his voice) is attested both by Mary Shelley and by E. J. Trelawney. Referring to *Shelley at Oxford*, Trelawney said, 'Hogg has painted Shelley exactly as I knew him'.[4] On the strength of this we can say that few poets have had their voices so fully and accurately described.

Hogg says that Shelley's voice was high or shrill in pitch, rapid in utterance, loud in volume, harsh in timbre, unmodulated in rhythm. Most people's voices rise in pitch and volume when excited or enthusiastic and they become more voluble. Undoubtedly Shelley, at the age of nineteen, was living at a fever pitch of enthusiasm and, even more than most nineteen-year-olds, he had much to say, much to exclaim about, much to be indignant at. He loved argument and, apart from T. J. Hogg, there must have been few, if any, at Oxford with whom he could have let himself go. But is it not exactly such a physical voice as Hogg described—shrill, rapid, often harsh and un-modulated, nearly always excited or enthusiastic—that, as readers, we hear behind the printed signs on the pages that go to make up the *Poetical Works of Shelley*? Or ought to hear? That we are forced to hear indeed unless those printed signs are to appear mad? That voice, which was unique—and descrip-tion, however accurate, can never present or even define, something unique—is now actually silent for ever; perpetually silent yet heard behind the silence of printed pages. In the absence of the original we at least demand of a reciter that he manage his voice so as to make it correspond with Shelley's (which we already hear with our inner ear) as nearly as possible; and, if we read aloud to ourselves, we should aim to echo, or imitate, the voice we hear with our inner ear, and have come to recognize as Shelley's, as nearly as possible. If this, it is argued, is to produce an unpleasant result because Shelley's voice was unpleasant, we can take comfort from Thomas Love Peacock. Peacock, discussing Hogg's *Shelley at Oxford*, wrote:

> There is a good deal in these volumes about Shelley's dis-cordant voice. This defect he certainly had; but it was chiefly observable when he spoke under excitement. Then his voice was not only dissonant, like a jarring strike, but he spoke in sharp fourths, the most unpleasing sequence of sound that can fall on human ear: but it was scarcely so when he spoke calmly, and not at all so when he read; on the contrary, he seemed then to have his voice under perfect command: it was good both in tune and tone; it was low and soft, but clear, distinct, and expressive. I have heard him read almost all Shakespeare's tragedies, and some of his more poetical comedies, and it was a pleasure to hear him read them.[1]

We can take comfort not, as Mr Sam Hynes and Mr Monroe C. Beardsley would have it[2] because the 'embodied voices' of the individual poems of Shelley, though various, are unrelated to the physical voice of the poet, but because the discordance of

---

[1] *The Halliford Edition of the Works of Thomas Love Peacock*, edited by H. F. B. Brett-Smith and C. E. Jones (Constable, 1934), vol. VIII, pp. 55–56.

[2] In the correspondence columns of *The Times Literary Supplement* of October 7, 1960.

his uncontrolled, when excited, speaking voice was resolved by metrical rhythm when he was reading. In fact the resolution of the tonal discordance, implicit to some extent in all other forms of utterance, is the essential function of rhythm—though with this resolution other results ensue, eminently this: the semantic content of the words is modified. Further, in rhythmical utterance the work of grammar and syntax ceases to be limited to pointing logical relations.

If Shelley read passages, or even whole plays, in a voice 'low and soft' it was because the rhythm of such passages (or of such and such a play) commanded such a 'tune and tone'. More broadly, the matter (of what?—of *Hamlet*?) commanded such a reading, and, in reading, Shelley echoed not his own very different voice but that of Shakespeare, or of those actors Shakespeare wrote for, in this or that play. 'Writing' his own voice, Shelley is mainly shrill, though the actual 'discordance' of the speaking voice is then satisfied or resolved rhythmically.

This is not to say that Shelley's voice remained constant. Between the ages of nineteen, when Hogg met him, and twenty-nine Shelley's voice probably changed after the manner that most male voices change. By 'after the manner' we mean that the voice of a man is not quite the same he had as a youth: that the voice of a man of twenty-nine is distinguishable from that of a first-year undergraduate. Shelley was scarcely less ardent in his convictions in 1822 than in 1811, but hopes are other than convictions, and his hopes had undergone seasoning. The ardour, initially temperamental, had probably become confirmed through his reading. But because Shelley's idealism did not turn into an acceptance of the established order of things, the end of most adolescents' revolutionary enthusiasm, it does not follow that his hopes of 'universal liberation' had not been chastened between his nineteenth and twenty-ninth years. Such a chastening really occurred. Besides, he suffered the suffering of disappointment, often and deeply, in other ways. This was experience, something that happens in time—in this case in a decade—and time or experience told on Shelley's voice as they do on other voices. The usual effect of time and of experience on the voice is to deepen it, increase its range of inflexions, and to make it slower in utterance. But Shelley's hope,

70

and he lived by hope, had not turned to despair by 1822. On the contrary, the hope had become heroic—graver, more patient, firmer, less conquerable. Mary Shelley puts the process thus: 'A very few years, with attendant events had checked the ardour of Shelley's hopes, though he still thought them well grounded, and that to advance their fulfilment was the noblest task man could achieve.'[1]

Shelley's voice altered with this checking to his hopes, and the evidence of the change is in the printed signs. Behind or within *The Triumph of Life* is heard the identical voice Hogg had heard at Oxford, but its qualities of shrillness, rapidity, loudness, monotony have been tempered. Hogg's description is still a generally exact description of the voice behind the *Poetical Works* as a whole, but that general description needs refinement according as to whether we are especially considering the earlier or later poetry.

ii

The voice of Shelley, which we hear in our minds when we read the printed work, and which we demand of a reciter or performer that he imitate, exactly suits the themes and events which occupy that work. Dizzy soarings, rapturous ascents, precipitous journeyings, aerial cars or chariots in speedy motion, careering clouds—these are typical events in the poetry, requiring for their rendering a high-pitched, rapid, ecstatic, and scarcely varied vocal delivery. Here are some lines, drawn at random, yet typical of Shelley; typical, that is, of the voice we hear declaiming them, typical of the voice required for their declamation:

> A course precipitous, of dizzy speed,
> Suspending thought and breath....[2]

This is one of many such journeys, and all the journeys are rapid and, because they are rapid, the scenery is swirled past

---

[1] Note to *Alastor* by Mrs Shelley, p. 30. References are to the large type Oxford Standard Authors edition of the *Poetical Works*.
[2] *The Revolt of Islam*, p. 42.

or, if the scenery is in fact static, it yet actually presents the illusion of hurrying past:

> The scene was changed, and away, away, away!
>   Thorough the air and over the sea we sped,
> And Cyntha in my sheltering bosom lay,
>   And the winds bore me—through the darkness spread
>   Around, the gaping earth then vomited
> Legions of foul and ghastly shapes, which hung
>   Upon my flight; and ever, as we fled,
>   They plucked at Cyntha—soon to me then clung
> A sense of actual things those monstrous dreams among.[1]

It is true that this last violent journey had succeeded a period of 'calm talk beneath the sphere / Of the calm mount'. But, whatever the importance of that interregnum of 'calm', no more space is accorded it than the two half-lines to say that it had occurred. Then 'suddenly' (naturally with Shelley it is 'suddenly'), the calm talk was interrupted by a 'nameless fear' and 'a rush of thronging feet'. Shortly after this journey he is again off—and upward:

> Over the utmost hill at length I sped,
> A snowy steep.[2]

Of course such journeys, etherial more than terrestrial, occur throughout Shelley's works, and whoever it is that is undertaking them, whether it is 'I'—Shelley himself in vision or dream—or one of Shelley's delegates, there is this relation between the traveller and the properties of the landscape: they usually sweep past in the opposite direction as the 'I' pursues its journey, hurrying to reach the 'end' of that journey. Also, it must be conceded, that after mounting, climbing, soaring, there is necessarily often a decline, a fall or flop: and then Shelley's spirits droop correspondingly and his vocal pitch lowers. Occasionally the forces, whether human or natural or supernatural, are not moving in contrary directions but the same, and the impression then is of the need to overtake. An obvious example is that of the West Wind impetuously driving leaf,

---

[1] *The Revolt of Islam*, p. 65.   [2] *Ibid.*, p. 79.

cloud or wave. Shelley would here, at one point, be one of the drivers. But here is another example:

> There steams a plume-uplifting wind
> Which drives them on their path, while they
>   Believe their own swift wings and feet
> The sweet desires within obey:
> And so they float upon their way,
> Until, still sweet, but loud and strong,
> The storm of sound is driven along,
>   Sucked up and hurrying . . . . [1]

Shelley, in short, weaving

> *swift* language from impassioned themes,[2]

like his 'typical' Skylark tends always to be climbing

> Higher still and higher.

As with this, so with the foregoing quotations, there is no doubt as to how they should be recited aloud—with a shrill, almost quivering ardour. A reader hears Shelley's voice hurrying, and rising, and aspiring. His voice in excitement approaches, yet avoids, a screech. The themes of his poetry, its imagery, its accidentals, all agree with his customary orientation of spirit— a forward-looking hope—that expresses itself, vocally, in a high-pitched excitement.[3]

iii

Wild careering journeys, aerial or aqueous, or—ambiguously—both, in chariot or boat, are principal events, *the* principal events even, in Shelley's poetry. Sometimes, as in *Alastor*, the boat which

> fled on
> With unrelaxing speed [4]

can follow a river which flows, marvellously, uphill; at other times, as in *The Revolt of Islam*, a boat can leave its element and sail 'Swift as a cloud between the sea and sky', but, whatever the vehicle, its course is 'precipitous with dizzy speed', whether

---

[1] *Prometheus Unbound*, p. 233.   [2] *Revolt of Islam*, p. 94.
[3] For a fuller account of Shelley's orientation of spirit, see 'Shelley and the Future Tense' in my *Poets' Grammar* (Routledge, 1958).
[4] *Ibid.*, p. 23.

in *The Daemon of the World*, in *Alastor*, in *The Revolt of Islam* or in *The Witch of Atlas*. Whenever the vehicle soars there is a crescendo of excitement and thrilled enthusiastic joy, a rise in Shelley's vocal pitch and an increase in the rapidity of his utterance. True, there are the intervals between such soarings, when the chariot or speeding boat stops, collapses or falls. But these occasions are briefly reported, are not dwelt on or realized. They are literal moments of dejection, and such moments are—to Shelley—anti-poetic. Such are states of dethronement, and they are but briefly reported because, however long they may endure, they are (to Shelley) states in which vision is impossible and in which poetry can neither be written nor conceived. Such a state of desertion is reported in the fourth section of the 'Ode to the West Wind', but the rest of the poem is a prayer for a deliverance from such a state and a record that the prayer has been answered. For Shelley the poetic or visionary state—'poetic' and 'visionary', with Shelley, are interchangeable—is contingent on possession by the 'Spirit of Delight' and that 'Spirit of Delight' depends on a condition of being which we must call hope, and a belief in that hope. The substance of the hope cannot indeed be presently possessed or actualized—or there would be no hope—but it must be genuinely attainable.

Shelley, then, is volatile, and beats 'luminous wings in the void', whether in vain or not is the responsibility of each single reader. Our immediate concern is the pitch and kind of projection of any human voice when expressing hope, and with Shelley's in particular.

For we are dealing with Shelley's principal, perhaps solitary, action—using 'action' in that neo-Aristotelian sense where it means not the *plot* of a poem or a play (for the plot is simply the externalization of the action), but the 'growth' or 'movement of the soul' undergone by the protagonist.[1] Shelley's action is not only abundantly graphed in figurative journeys—figurative, because the journeys are psychic journeys—by flying boat, car or chariot in such poems as *The Daemon of the World*, *Alastor*, *The Revolt of Islam* or *The Witch of Atlas*, but it is apparent everywhere in his poetry. The action had to take place, indeed, if Shelley was to create at all; the alternative was a literal

[1] The dependence on Francis Fergusson (see his *The Idea of a Theatre*) for this reading of 'action' will be clear.

dejection. Hence, outside the poems we have mentioned, the *literal* informing motion of 'insurrection' in *Prometheus Unbound*; hence the leaping, and so delighted, fountains of 'Arethusa'; hence the peculiar appropriateness—in vocal terms, vocally rendered—of 'The Skylark'; hence the force of such constitutive lines of imagery in *Adonais* as

He has outsoared the shadow of our night;

and hence the necessity of the line by line imagery of Shelley's greatest poem, 'Ode to the West Wind'. But why does Shelley *literally* speak thus? Why must we read aloud his poetry, or hear it being declaimed by Shelley, the way we do? Why is the substance of his poetry uniquely matched to his physical voice? The forward-looking and careering journeys were, as we have said, psychical or symbolical journeys, but why do they require the idioms of height and rapid movement?

Attempts to answer the questions lead us to the insoluble mystery of perhaps all idioms, but particularly of the idioms—certainly not particularly Shelley's, but rather universal—expressing elation, confidence, joy, hope. Shelley's poetry, as his most hostile critic has observed, is 'leaning forwards'. Well, why is the idiom '*looking* forward' expressed by, or applied to, people who are in the happy state of hope? Why 'look forward'? Since they do not literally look forward, it is a metaphor. But it is a metaphor that has been adopted as being exactly true—apter than any literal statement. Shelley's poetry, even as it rises, *looks forward*.

Shelley's poetry not only 'looks forward'—looks forward, for hope necessarily only operates in the Future Tense—but it 'looks up'. 'Looks up': again I quote an idiom that is yet exactly descriptive of Shelley's imagery. Why 'looks up'? Let us consider these idioms, sayings which because of their expressive truth have been accepted as idioms, of up- and downness, and relate them to vocal pitch and to Shelley's poetry.

In English, when a man is prospering we say, 'He's on the way *up*'; if he's failing, we say, 'He's on the way *down*' or 'He's on the *down*ward path'. These are not literally true statements but they are metaphorically true. If a young man is ambitious we say, 'He is aiming *high*'. We might say of another man that he marries '*beneath* himself'. Or someone, to an enquiry as to his well-being might reply, 'I'm feeling on top of the world'. The metaphor for success, joy or health is one of *height*: yet the metaphor may have a bodily or mental basis—the man may really feel that he is in 'the ascendant' or that his 'spirits are soaring'. Now, in contrast, a person is 'feeling low'; another is 'down in the dumps'; a third is 'so-so', i.e. neither high nor low. To what extent are these idiomatic 'high's' and 'low's' literal, and to what extent metaphorical?[1] And should we forbear to enquire whether metereological forecasts of 'high pressure', of 'high temperature', of 'low troughs of depression' (or even the 'top' and 'bottom' of a school form) are more metaphorical or more literal in that they suggest some sort of a notched tally-stick held vertically?

This metaphor of height (in 'high spirits', in 'low spirits'; he reached the 'summit' of his profession, or 'the top of the tree') and depth, to express conditions of emotional health or worldly status, is not, of course, peculiar to English, but is common (I am led to believe) to all languages. The 'Slough of Despond' is Bunyan, is Biblical English, but also Biblical any other language—including the original Hebrew. Heaven is *above*, hell is *below*, in all languages except those we know nothing about. In all cultures a king is 'raised up' among his people, and in all cultures slaves and suitors 'bow down' or 'abase' themselves.

A man is down-cast in English, *abbatu* in French, and dejected in Latin. Fortunes are 'overthrown' or 'built up' in all languages; and behind the Latinisms 'exalted', 'elated', 'eminent', on the one hand, and 'disgraced', 'suppressed', 'depressed' and 'dejected', on the other, there is a residual height–depth metaphor and/or literal meaning no less real than in the Anglo-Saxon 'down-trodden' or 'at the bottom'. But these are but comments on idioms which seem so rooted in human nature that few people have paused to ponder on their rationale or to question whether such idioms will be still viable in, say, the age

---

[1] 'In Tube lift hearing the phrase "fed up", and realizing that all our analogies spiritual and intellectual are derived from purely physical acts. Nay more, all attributes of the absolute and the abstract are really nothing more (in so far as they mean anything) but elaborations of simple passions.'
'All poetry is an affair of the body—that is, to be real it must affect body.' A jotting by T. E. Hulme—*Speculations* (Routledge & Kegan Paul, ed. 1960) p. 242.

of the New Physics. And, finally, we point out that when we say Shelley's, or anybody's, voice 'goes up' or 'goes down', that 'up' and 'down' are (strictly) metaphorical; that 'alto' is meta-phorical, and so is 'bass'.[1]

Yet Shelley's voice is keyed *up*. Accepting that the metaphor has ingrafted itself into all languages of which we have know-ledge, we are next bound to recognize that when a man is *excited* his voice is 'high' and that when he is *depressed* it is 'low'. Recognizing this, we realize how Shelley's poetry should sound aloud, and in realizing this we recover the pitch and timbre of his physical voice long after his death. We realize that when, in the 'Ode to the West Wind' (1819), he prays,

> Oh, lift me as a wave, a leaf, a cloud!
> I fall upon the thorns of life! I bleed!
>
> A heavy weight of hours has chained and bowed
> One too like thee: tameless, and swift, and proud.

that the figures or metaphors of up-ness and down-ness are neither peculiar to Shelley nor to English. He is, or rather has been, 'low' and he prays to be 'lifted' and, that he was 'lifted', even in the act of confessing his past lowness, we must fairly suppose. By the end of the poem he is thoroughly well exalted, exalted enough to satisfy anyone—the poet or his readers. But, we also note, in the lines just quoted, that the pitch line or con-tour of the voice (Shelley's or our own in rightly hearing him) coincides with the pitch line of the meaning—the rise and fall imagery, the statements of soaring or decline. The voice rises in sympathy with the wish, hope or substance of the prayer, 'Oh, lift me . . .', and it expresses the ascending order of the planes, indicated by

> Oh, lift me as a wave, a leaf, a cloud!

in that the voice accordingly raises pitch in succession for 'wave', 'leaf', 'cloud', only to slump again for

> I fall upon the thorns of life! I bleed!
>
> A heavy weight of hours has chained and bowed
> One too like thee. . . .

---

[1] I am indebted to a colleague, H. D. Rankin, for a stimulating conversa-tion on the subject of the history of the Latin prepositions *sub* and *de*.

Yet the fall is in fact preparatory to the ascending vocal pitch of Section V, which is so thoroughly satisfying and Shelleian in every way; which is representative of his 'action' (or 'movement or thrust of soul') in that it ends in a blazon of joyful triumph, the triumph of Shelley's apotheosis and a general *up*rising of all peoples. He ends *up*, up in the vocal scale, keen-eyed and visionary. Shelley's action, or theme of soaring, which is figured in the imagery, is exactly suited to his voice; but his action, or theme, is universal in that we all, as common idioms and figures in every language reveal, are habituated to the metaphor whose sense is emphasized by vocal pitch—when it is rendered aloud—of up- and down-ness.

And the forward-looking? A living for the future, a mortgaging of the present, a denial that it contains the best or highest goods, is constitutional to Shelley and endemic among humanity. Recollection of a past, the recollection of any past, is a sad affair if only—especially if it were a joyful past—because of the realization that it *is* past (hence the vowel pitch of *The Prelude* is low even when it tells of the most moving events—the events of the poem are all past, are revived in memory only); but that the future must be better is the sustaining belief (or illusion) of everyone who 'lives in hope'. We take the idiom 'to live in hope' literally, for not to hope is to despair, and to despair is to commit suicide, or to be a Thomas Hardy whose one joy, and so motive for life, is expressing the death of hope. But Shelley lived in hope, and hence the characteristic verb-form of his poetry is the Future Tense. Since what was to happen in the future was thrilling, Shelley's voice thrills with the happiness of anticipation. Like the medieval Mystery Cycles *Prometheus Unbound* spans all time; but though the opening situation is lodged in the remote past, and the middle acts take place in a present extended beyond our own time, past and present eagerly incline towards that millenium which is overtaken in the last act. Until the prophecy of that last act is achieved, through the slow historical process, we are told to hope

> till Hope creates
> From its own wreck the thing it contemplates.

iv

Shelley's voice had been as Hogg described it but, as Mary Shelley said, 'a very few years had checked the ardour of his hopes'. Towards the end of his life, indeed, a low vocal key to match low spirits is heard in such complaints as 'A Widow Bird', 'Lines written among the Euganean Hills', 'To the Moon' and in other fragments—fragments where the euphoria, a condition which was necessary to Shelley for confident and complete acts of composition, was absent. Nevertheless, as Mary Shelley also said, Shelley still thought his 'hopes' (an application of the concept of hope is essential to any understanding of Shelley) 'well-grounded', and that 'to advance their fulfilment was the noblest task man could achieve'. A deepening of Shelley's voice, while nevertheless it preserved its individual character, that accompanied—and expressed—the checking of his hopes' ardour, is evident in *The Triumph of Life*, the poem on which he was working when he was drowned.

This poem is incomplete. In fact, the lines that survive constitute merely the beginning of an allegory. What is remarkable, apart from the excellence of the verse, the assured mastery of the *terza rima*,[1] is an alteration in Shelley's voice following the reversal of his customary symbol—the car or chariot is here not to be a vehicle for a celestial or transcendental tour but, instead, a juggernaut grinding out the life of humanity. True, the poem starts off in the typical Shelley way:

> Swift as a spirit hastening to his task
> Of glory and of good, the Sun sprang forth
> Rejoicing in his splendour, and the mask
>
> Of darkness fell from the awakened Earth. . . .

Here is the Shelleian rapidity and crescendo yet, as the poem proceeds, one is struck, not only by a Dantesque precision, an eye for particulars, but by a new severity and depth of vocal tone.

Having established the hope—it is implicit in the title that Life is to emerge triumphant in the end, an end never to be reached—the poem proceeds with Shelley bringing in his

[1] T. S. Eliot drew attention to this mastery in the special Dante number of *The Sewanee Review*, Winter 1952.

heretofore favourite symbol of the car, but reversing its meaning. The reversal indicates a conversion rather than a simple development. But they need not be regarded as opposites. Such a mutation is marked by a change of vocal tone. The altered, and yet identical, voice bespeaks a world of disappointment that is yet contained by a belief that is a hope. He brings in his car but with a new-old purpose. In the old purpose the car was air-borne so as to give the rapturous Shelley a vista of the radiant future and to capture it before it arrived in time. In this new purpose the car is brought in, but it is a juggernaut:

> The chariot rolled, a captive multitude
> Was driven;—all those who had grown old in power
> Or misery,—all who had their age subdued
>
> By action or by suffering, and whose hour
> Was drained to its last sand in weal or woe. . .

In this new purpose, the car or chariot is the necessary and not-to-be-opposed or avoided record and vehicle of the past. It is history. The car heretofore in time has been misguided. But so, the implicit judgment warrants this, has Shelley been misguided in thinking his own previous charioteers easily successful. The poet has acquired an historical sense, looks backward now as well as forward, and his poetry has to be read, and heard, in a new way—if only because the word 'chariot' is no longer a signal for excited shrillness and a rapturous prospect.

The reading of Shelley, whether aloud, or silently yet so as to hear, demands of the reader an act of audial empathy. To experience Shelley we must inhabit his voice. The marks on the page are merely *signs for* that voice. In Shelley's last year of life his voice changed. If we have sufficient vocal imagination to hear, so as to imitate, his earlier voice, then we will be able to enact—within ourselves—that change in his being which was conditional for the composition of the opening of *The Triumph of Life*.

In the course of this chapter, and of its predecessor, we have affirmed that the typical tense of Shelley is a Future or a Future Conditional, and that the typical tense of Tennyson is a Perfect or a Perfect Conditional.

Obviously what we do *not* mean is that Shelley always uses the inflections of a Future Indicative (so that he actually says 'Mankind *will become* free'), though they are common; or that Tennyson consistently employs the inflexions of a Past or a Pluperfect Conditional ('If only it had been that Hallam had not died'). The numerically predominant verb inflexions in both poets is the Present whenever they are expressing their *now* feelings and not narrating the long past as in *Idylls of the King*. For, as with all poets, the important tense for Shelley and Tennyson is the tense of their *now*, the now of their respective poems. Hence the one says

> I bring fresh showers to the thirsting flowers . . .

and the other

> The long day wanes, the slow moon climbs, the deep
> Moans round with many voices . . .

But though Shelley's 'bring' or Tennyson's 'wanes', 'climbs', 'moans', are alike offering themselves as Presents, the Present 'bring' of Shelley and the Present group of Tennyson belong, in fact, to quite different *nows*, to happenings now. And the difference is not just a difference between a general and a specific Present, the difference between 'the cloud is now actually condensing' and 'moons wane' (as a recurrently true statement), but a difference rather between Shelley's *now* of desire or hope and Tennyson's *now* of memory. Shelley is projecting himself into the future so that it is no longer a future to him but a present. One is a poet of avid desire, the other a poet of regret. 'If I were a dead leaf thou mightest bear, / If I were a swift cloud to fly with thee . . .', prays Shelley in the 'Ode to the West Wind', and, before the poem is out—very soon, in fact—Shelley *is* a 'leaf', more, a whole forest, and what had lain ahead of him in time when he expressed his wish becomes, by the end of the poem, actualized. What had been Future becomes Present. Contrast Tennyson's 'I would that my tongue could utter / The thoughts that arise in me'. The thoughts arise from the memory of 'the tender grace of a day that is dead', and to that 'day that is dead' he transfers his *now*. His actual present loses itself in that past both in this poem and in *In Memoriam*, and it is not sufficient to say that in *Ulysses* the moon 'wanes' because Tennyson is writing a dramatic monologue and is using there a Historic or dramatic Present. Rather, he prefers to live in the past and so make it his present. The *now* of the Present inflexions, in the poetry of Shelley, when looked at closely, is a Future, and the *now* of Tennyson is a Perfect or Pluperfect. The actual tensal inflexions *in* their poems are modified by the expressly stated or assumed tense of the poems themselves. In the case of Shelley the containing tense of his poems, modifying local inflexions, is a Future Conditional which becomes Present Indicative through the action of the poem (*Prometheus Unbound*, etc.) ; and in the case of Tennyson it is a Pluperfect reporting an event that ought never to have happened except for the eventually conceded 'It is better to have loved and lost / Than never loved at all'. For I take it that 'hope' and 'desire' are the typical acts of the mind or heart looking forwards and that 'remorse' or 'regret' are the typical acts of the mind or heart looking backwards.

What there is to add here is this: we cannot finally tell how much the physical voices of Shelley and Tennyson acted on their temperaments and experiences, or *vice versa*, but we can point to results. In the results the poetry of Shelley requires for its saying (and hearing) one kind of voice which Shelley had, and the poetry of Tennyson requires for its saying (and hearing) a quite other kind of voice which Tennyson had.

Each voice defines itself by its choice of themes and imagery, by its choice of phonic elements to provide the equivalents in sound of such themes and imagery, and by the choice of those grammatical forms and constructions requiring an appropriate vocal inflexion.

VI The Voice of Milton

WHEN Milton was a young man he composed these lines:

> Haste thee nymph, and bring with thee
> Jest and youthful Jollity,
> Quips and Cranks, and wanton Wiles,
> Nods, and Becks, and Wreathed Smiles . . .;

when he was no longer young, but rather deep in middle life, he dictated such lines as these:

> He scarce had ceas't when the superiour Fiend
> Was moving toward the shore; his ponderous shield
> Ethereal temper, massy, large and round
> Behind him cast. . . .

The question, to frame it in simple terms, is: In what ways had Milton's personal, or physical, voice changed or altered, since he was a young man to enable him to compose and sound aloud in his mind (not, indeed, to write) and then sound again in the act of dictation, such lines as these from *Paradise Lost*?

Cleanth Brooks and John Edward Hardy observe: 'With the major poems [meaning *Paradise Lost, Paradise Regained* and *Samson Agonistes*] Milton's style changes.'[1] To what extent, if any, does this change of 'style' reflect—or, better, bespeak or echo—a change in Milton's personal, or physical, voice which

---

[1] *Poems of Mr John Milton:* the 1645 Edition. Ed. C. Brooks and J. E. Hardy, New York, 1951.

had taken place since the period of the early, or so-called minor, poems?

Or: Did Milton's voice change? If so, is the evidence of this change discernible in the printed marks on the pages that go to make up what are called Milton's 'Poetical Works'?

Put it how we may, subordinate (hardly subordinate in importance: they 'depend' only in logic. In the result they are at least equal in importance) questions start up. Could Milton have written otherwise than his voice, and the development of that voice, urged him? Can we recover that voice so as to hear it, in the obvious absence of gramophone records, from the printed signs alone—helped, perhaps, by the descriptions of his friends or early biographers?

It will be realized that we will have to depend almost entirely on the printed signs. Not that his friends and early biographers say nothing on the subject of his voice, but because—as it must be conceded—no description of a voice, however detailed or vivid, can be more than circumstantial or circumlocutory, can be more than about and about, for the simple and final reason that each and every voice is unique. Such descriptions therefore are customarily metaphorical. The general fact can be stated; the unique truth requires metaphor. We cannot precisely identify a voice from description until we actually hear it. But when we have heard it, then we know it indeed; yet know it for the first time. Nevertheless, I think we can reconstruct the personal voice of Milton in our inner hearing from the printed signs alone. Still, let us first mark what the contemporaries and early biographers tell us.

John Aubrey's 'minutes', dated 1681, constitute the earliest recollections of Milton founded on personal interview. Aubrey has often been charged with being credulous and unreliable— and has as often been defended. But that this inimitable master of the vivid and telling phrase had been in Milton's company and had stood beside or near him, is 'clinched'—as Miss Helen Darbishire puts it—by the following: 'He was scarce as high as I am (*Quaere*, Quot feet am I high? *Resp.* Of middle Stature.'[1] As far as his reminiscences of Milton are concerned, at any rate, Aubrey is not only delightful but also trustworthy. Now in

[1] *The Early Lives of Milton* edited by Helen Darbishire (Constable), 1932, p. xi.

these 'minutes' we find observations concerning Milton's voice:

> Extreme pleasant in his conversation, & at dinner, supper &c: but Satyricall. He pronounced ye letter R very hard a certain signe of a Satyricall Witt fr. Jo: Dreyden.

> He had a delicate tuneable Voice & had good skill: his father instructed him: he had an Organ in his house: he played on that most.[1]

In the margin against the note recounting Milton's way of pronouncing the letter R, Aubrey has written 'Littera canina'. Presumably R is 'the dog letter' because when rolled or, as Milton would have it, 'rowld', or when pronounced 'very hard', it resembles a dog's growl or snarl. To an objection that Aubrey has described not Milton's voice but his pronunciation of one letter, one could answer that a certain kind of temperament, of 'Witt', selects a certain kind of pronunciation (as Dryden indicated), or that a voice is given 'character' by just such an idiosyncrasy.

Aubrey's 'minutes' might seem to amount to no more than a general commendation of Milton's 'tuneable voice', 'excellent ear' and skill in music, both vocal and instrumental. As far as instrumental music is concerned, there is the testimony of John Phillips, the younger of Milton's nephews: 'he play'd much upon an Organ he kept in the House'.[2] Phillips also said of his uncle: 'Hee had an excellent Ear, and could bear a part both in Vocal & Instrumental Music.'[3] In support of this Anthony à Wood, though drawing on the materials supplied him by Aubrey, says of Milton: 'He had a delicate, tuneable voice, an excellent ear, could play on the Organ, and bear a part in vocal and instrumental Musick';[4] while the Jonathan Richardsons, father and son, observe 'His Voice was Musically Agreeable'.[5]

The evidence of these men amount to little, but that little is important. The importance consists in just this: the early

---

[1] *The Early Lives of Milton* edited by Helen Darbishire (Constable), 1932, p. 6.
[2] From John Toland's *Life*, 1698. *Ibid.*, p. 194.   [3] *Ibid.*, p. 32.
[4] From *Fasti Oxonienses*, 1691, *Ibid.*, p. 48.   [5] *Life*, 1734, *Ibid.*, p. 204.

biographers tell us exactly what we would have expected had we been ignorant of the existence of such tributes—that Milton had a conscious musician's ear, a conscious musician's voice (it was 'tuneable', i.e. it was obedient to Milton's will and knowledge of musical effects) and that, in his latter years, he played an organ.

Why might we have supposed as much as we are, in fact, told? Because we had so inferred from our own listening to Milton in his poetry. In the process we had constructed—so as later to assume—a personality with just such gifts, and with just such a voice, as his biographers report. From our experience of him, we had expected Milton, above all poets, to be conscious—perhaps overconscious—of controlled or manipulated sound.

That Milton, who had a 'tuneable voice', also had a fastidious and cunning ear (hearing and speaking are intimately connected activities), is attested, for example, by an anecdote related by Thomas Elwood, in his autobiography. Elwood, a Quaker, a man of mature years, ashamed at his lack of humane learning, had been granted the privilege of attending Milton, and reading under his direction: 'He [Milton] perceiving with what earnest Desire I pursued Learning, gave me not only all the Encouragement, but all the Help he could. For, having a curious Ear, he understood by my Tone when I understood what I read, and when I did not: and accordingly would stop me, Examine me, and open the most difficult Passages to me.'[1]

Elwood here refers to an occasion in 1661, when Milton was quite blind and *Paradise Lost* about half or three-quarters done. Elwood had been reading a Latin author aloud to Milton, and had first been corrected for using English pronunciation. Milton had then expounded to Elwood the principles of the Continental or Italian system of sounding Latin, probably on the lines of his *Letter of Education*, where Latin 'is to be fashion'd to a distinct and cleer pronunciation, as neer as may be to the *Italian*, expecially in the vowels. For we Englishmen being farre Northerly, do not open our mouthes in the cold air, wide enough to grace a Southern tongue; but are observ'd by all other nations to speak exceeding close and inward. So that to

[1] Quoted in *Life*, 1734, p. lv.

smatter Latin with an English mouth, is as ill hearing as law French.'[1]

Elwood was told to 'open his mouth' and doubtless he did, or tried to; but, thanks to his 'curious Ear', Milton knew by the 'Tone' when it was that Elwood understood the Latin author he was reading aloud and when he did not. To this it might be said that we all have, to a greater or lesser extent, a 'curious Ear', and that we infer from the 'Tone' when it is that a speaker or reader understands what he says—or reads—and when he does not. Especially, it might be argued, does a blind man rely on a heightened sensitivity to speech-tones—and Milton was blind. Precisely. Milton, all his life conscious or overconscious to sound values, necessarily became more conscious after his blindness. This naturally leads us to an anecdote preserved by the Jonathan Richardsons:

> Musick he Lov'd Extreamly, and Understood Well. 'tis said he Compos'd, though nothing of That has been brought down to Us. he diverted Himself with Performing, which they say he did Well on the Organ and Bas-Viol. and This was a great Relief to him after he had lost his Sight.
>
> in relation to his Love of Musick, and the Effect it had upon his Mind, I remember a Story I had from a Friend I was Happy in for many Years, and who lov'd to talk of *Milton*, as he Often Did. *Milton* hearing a Lady Sing Finely, *'now will I Swear'* (says he) This Lady is Handsom.' his Ears were Eyes to Him.[2]

That 'his Ears were Eyes to him', that he came to be enclosed in a world of sound, and that he communicated and pronounced on this world in his own voice which echoed that sound, has been implicit in the critical attacks on Milton's prestige since 1930, and indeed before that date. But we aim here at making what has been implicit explicit, and thereby to convert the basis of reproach to a positive—to show that what has been held as a limitation was in fact the condition of achievement.

The early biographers, while they remember and pay tribute to Milton's 'tuneable voice', necessarily fail to define that voice: necessarily because Milton's voice was unique, and everything that is unique, unless it can be weighed and measured, resists definition. Nevertheless the general descriptions of Milton's

---

[1] Quoted in *Life*, 1734, p. lvii.   [2] *Ibid.*, p. 204.

voice offered us by the early biographers possess a value—they corroborate what we had supposed from our own reading of the poetry. That poetry indeed appears under the guise of printed signs. It may be objected that print cannot alone record the parameters of a voice. But meaning and rhythm help to point those features. Further, there is Milton's idiosyncratic orthography, pointing and capitalization.

Now the peculiarities of Milton's spelling, punctuation and use of capitals engaged the interest of an early biographer as revelatory of the manner in which Milton *pronounced and sounded*[1] language. This biographer was the elder Jonathan Richardson, by profession a painter. Richardson never met Milton but was intimate with some of those who had. He knew Milton vicariously and he loved the man and the poet. The passage now to be quoted is probably well-known; but it is so central to the argument that little apology is needed for presenting it in full. Apart from its immediate relevance, what it has to say has clearly an application to the work of all other poets who lived and spoke and wrote before the standardization of orthography and punctuation:

What has been alleg'd as Probabilities, appears in Fact to be Certain. That the Original MS. was of the Hand-Writing of Several is Agreed, but does That appear by the Printed Book? Nothing Less; 'tis Uniform Throughout: it must have then been Revis'd and Corrected by Some one, Directed at least, and that This was *Milton* himself is Evident by its Exact Conformity with his Spelling and Pointing in What he Publish'd when he had his Sight; as also with his Other Works after That was gone. for full Satisfaction, Those that please may have recourse to Those Works, the Original Editions, for They are to be had. in the Mean time if they will give Me Credit, they will be Assured, that not only the Printing is Equally Accurate with what is to be found in Any of them, but 'tis rather More so than in most of the rest. as indeed 'tis of more Importance, that it should be Just Here than in Any of his Other Works, as 'tis his Principal One, and That in which even the Points Direct and Determine the Sense most Often and most Remarkably. We have found, in Several Instances, that what seem'd at first Sight to be the True One, was far Inferiour to what

[1] I am not, of course, using the words 'pronounced' and 'sounded' as equivalents. But see pp. 30–32 above.

was indeed So, but would not have been Discover'd, unless by following Those Guides, Almost Universally Faithful.

There are Some Peculiarities in the Spelling of certain Words in *Paradise Lost*, not by Accident, but from One End to the Other; the Same is in what he Wrote with his Own Hand Years before to go into a Detail of These would be Dry to the Reader, nor is it Agreeable to Me; but One remarkable Instance I will give: the Word *Their* in This Poem, as in Many of his Writings, is *Thir*. What led him This way of Spelling this Word I know not, though long Before *Paradise Lost*. 'tis not an Ancient Way of Writing, it was Always *Their* or *Theyr*.

Several Other Particularities of This Kind are to be found in *Milton's* Works, Which let any One peruse, they will be Convinc'd that there is Such a Similitude of Spelling between Those Published when he was Blind, and Those Before, that shows they *were All under the same Direction*. Had we known it Otherwise the Author would not have been suspected to be Blind by Any want of Exactness in This.

In *Paradise Lost* Care has been taken of the Orthography where the Sense was in no Danger, and meerly for the sake of Accuracy; as in the Word *Scent* Thus Always Spelt, to distinguish it from *Sent*. To Smell is *Sentir* (Fr.) *Sentire* (It.) Thence we have *Scent*, but as no *c* is in the Word we borrow from Milton rejects it. So the Word *Rhime* being deriv'd from *Rhythmos* (Gr.) signifying (as *Milton* Himself has explain'd it) *Apt Numbers, fit Quantity of Syllables, and the Sense Variously drawn out from One Verse into Another;* and we having Made the same Word to stand for *the jingling Sound of Like Endings*, He has Distinguish'd the Different Ideas by Spelling the latter without the *h*. This is of Consequence, the Sense of the place not being Always Sufficient to keep the Reader from Confounding those Ideas. This Difference in the Spelling of these Words is seen in the short Discourse concerning the Verse in the first Quarto Edition, That of 68 or 69, and the Octavo of 74, I. 16. the Neglect of This in the Edition of 78, the First after the Author's Death, was the First Corruption that crept into the Copies of this Poem, and which has been follow'd by More, particularly in the Pointing, which consequently has also Sometimes Corrupted, Sometimes Perplexed the Sense; not but that Words also have been Chang'd, though indeed but Rarely, the Spelling Frequently; *Sent, Thir, Perfet, Then,* (when a Comparative) *Soule, Eeven, Minde, Don, Burden,* &c. All Moderniz'd and Spelt as Now.

in *Paradise Lost* there is a Remarkable Proof of Care which we have not Observ'd in any of our Author's Other Works, or Those of any Other Writer, and that is, the Words *He, we, me, ye,* are with a Double or a Single *e*, as the Emphasis lies upon them, or does not.¹ We could produce a great Number of Instances of This. Take only Two, II. 1021-2-3. VI. 286, 288. Nay, a Neglect of This kind is put into the Errata of the First Edition, the Fault is in II. 414, but the Second Edition has happen'd to Overlook it, though Otherwise Exceedingly Correct.²

Richardson, after giving further instances designed to show that the punctuation and spelling of the 1674 edition are indeed Milton's—the result of Milton's exacting directions to his scribes³ (each mark of punctuation and each idiosyncratic spelling representing how Milton thought he sounded to others, certainly how he sounded to himself)—concludes, 'All kinds of Verses have Sounds of their Own' and certainly Milton's has its 'Peculiar Musick' . . . so that his 'Ictus, or Cadence, or Musick bears . . . towards Somthing of his Own, by his Own Ear'.⁴

His 'Peculiar Musick', the consequence of his peculiar voice, was recognized not only by Milton's earliest readers, and

¹ If Richardson had read Donne's *Songs and Sonets* he would have found the weak and emphatic forms of these pronouns distinguished from each other. Incidentally, does not Richardson's own highly individual spelling, punctuation and use of capitals reveal aspects of his personality—by closely recording his speech—which would be obscured by the modern standard systems?

To save the reader the trouble of turning up Richardson's examples, here they are—the fault in II. 414 duly corrected:

> So he with difficulty and Labour hard
> Mov'd on, with difficulty and labour hee;
> But hee once past . . .
>> (II, 1020-3.)

> Unvanquisht, easier to transact with mee
> That thou shouldst hope, imperious, & with threats
> To chase me hence?
>> (VI, 286-288.)

> Here he had need
> All circumspection, and wee now no less
> Choice in our suffrage.
>> (II, 413-415.)

² *The Early Lives of Milton*, pp. 303-305.

³ That it was Edward Phillips who was primarily responsible for 'Correction as to the Orthography and Pointing' is suggested of course in his biography, *op. cit.*, p. 73. Indeed, it was the Miltonic spelling of certain words like 'thir' which enabled Miss Darbishire to identify the author of another biography of Milton as John Phillips, the poet's other nephew.

⁴ *Ibid.*, p. 311.

realized by Milton himself, in his poetry. It was heard, we are told, even behind or through his prose: 'So Early as when he Wrote for Divorce, though he Conceal'd his Name his Hand was known—*My Name I did not Publish* (says He) *as not willing it should Sway the Reader either For me or Against me, but when I was told that the Style, which what it Ails to be so soon distinguishable, I cannot tell, was known by most Men* . . .'[1]

Milton says his authorship was apparent from the *style* of the pamphlet, and we are generally ready to agree with the aphorism *le style est l'homme*. But what is 'style' but an individual, and so identifiable, mode? A writer's style is customarily conceived of as an individual, and so identifiable, mode of handling language as it appears on the printed page, and that in turn implies an individual mode of thinking and feeling, etc. 'A style' has therefore become synonymous with 'a private idiom'. But the 'style' of an actual speech, of any oral delivery, is as much conditioned by the speaker's voice as by his choice of language and his individual manner of thinking and feeling. Indeed, it can control his choice of language, his manner of thinking and feeling, his rhythms. *How* he speaks shapes *what* he speaks—where listeners are concerned. Thus a man tends to confine himself, in actual speech, to what his voice allows him most effectively to utter, and what that is he has learned from experience. So he repeats himself—more or less—and it is this repetition (none other than a self-ordained limitation) which gives him an identifiable personality for his friends to recognize. But if it be conceded, as far as ordinary conversation is concerned, that *how* the man speaks is as important as *what* he speaks (and that the *how* influences the *what*),[2] the question next follows: To what extent can 'vocal peculiarity'—the *how*—be preserved when the conversation is recorded in printed signs? The question, ranging far beyond verbatim newspaper reports, obviously includes the dialogue of characters in novels. Most would agree that in Dickens' novels many of the characters can be *heard* speaking; this is especially true of the highly eccentric characters. The reader creates in his auditory imagination

[1] *The Early Lives of Milton*, p. 315.
[2] That the *what* influences the *how* is assumed, but, as a proposition, it has been discussed more often than its reverse. It is the reverse that is my concern in this section on Milton, Shelley and Tennyson.

a voice to *fit* what is being so oddly said. A *how* is created to fit the *what*. That readers, out of their shared experience of a book, will agree as to the *how* can be tested whenever anyone is persuaded to read Dickens aloud to an audience. The audience will agree as to whether the dialogue is rendered well or ill, and will agree in what respects it was rendered well or ill, will agree with Dickens—that is—as to the exact tone, timbre, pitch of the voice required. What is true of Dickens' eccentric characters when they are talking is also true—though less grossly—of Jane Austen's non-eccentric young women: for in *Persuasion* we hear *how* Anne Elliot speaks while reading *what* she speaks.

But if it is true that the *how*, the vocal peculiarity, can survive transmission from actual speaking to silent print nowadays, it would be still truer of periods of the past—even bearing in mind the recent revival of oral entertainment on a large scale brought about by broadcasting, whether sound or television, and the long-playing 'high-fidelity' record. That the written and spoken language have steadily grown more divergent, so as almost to have become two separate instruments, is a matter of common doctrine and common knowledge, which must be accepted, although with the large reserves of the kind—the instances of Dickens' and Jane Austen's characters—I have indicated. But in Milton's time we are still within the living bounds of the great 'oral tradition'.

That phrase includes so much that perhaps I may be forgiven if I recall some of its implications. We are to be aware of a society and tradition where men and women still tried to write as they spoke; where men and women did not spell according to fixed authoritative standards, but according to the sound and feel the word had for them when they spoke it; when men and women punctuated, not according to the taught rules of syntax and grammar (to Latin rules, the truth of which, when applied to English psychology and sensory experience, can be fairly questioned), but according to their natural habits of breathing, phrasing and inflecting. We are within a tradition where the distribution of printed books was exceedingly thin and where the means of obtaining and communicating information, necessary or unnecessary, was not the newspaper, but by listening—by listening to the man in the pulpit, to the man in the Law Court, to the man in Parliament, to the man on the scaffold. We are in a tradition where entertainment had been once supplied from the boards of the theatre, and where the only verbal entertainment still to be enjoyed depended on securing someone to sing or to read aloud; we are in a tradition where few could read, and those who could did not read silently but moved their lips and repeated the words of their author, imitating or echoing his voice. We are in a tradition where no poet wrote but in expectation of being performed aloud before a few auditors at least, and the poet (especially the poet, though this applies even to the prose-writer too) consequently—and from natural and constitutional habit—composed as though he were being heard.

The elder Richardson says: 'There is Something in Every Man's whereby he is known, as by his Voice. . . .'[1] Richardson, it is true, goes on to say that what was peculiar about Milton, what betrayed his authorship of the pamphlet, was his 'Vigour', but the 'Vigour', being the distinguishing property of the 'style', was itself a property of Milton's personal voice.

ii

The exact date of *l'Allegro*, and so of its companion piece, *Il Penseroso*, is unknown. But whether composed at a late stage in Milton's career at Cambridge, as E. M. W. Tillyard argues,[2] or, subsequently, during the Horton period, *l'Allegro* is clearly an early poem. It might be objected that in selecting *l'Allegro* as representative of a young voice I am being unfair in that Milton is nowhere else so light-hearted, and that the theme of the exercise—it will be agreed that *l'Allegro* is an exercise—compelled a light touch. *L'Allegro* is, for Milton, even as an early poem, 'light', despite Dr Johnson's remark, 'The chearfulness is without levity'. I shall hope to meet this objection later, but in passing point out that the objection, in employing a metaphor derived from *weight* and *weighing* ('light-hearted', 'light touch', 'levity') to establish itself, involves us in a question central to this book. Why 'light'?[3]

[1] *The Early Lives of Milton*, p. 315.
[2] See *The Miltonic Setting* (Chatto & Windus, 1949), pp. 1–28.
[3] But the metaphor always seems apt, e.g.:

> Com, knit hands, and beat the ground,
> In a *light* fantastick round.
>
> *Comus*, 143–144.

Dr Tillyard assures us that *l'Allegro* and *Il Penseroso* were both composed for oral delivery to an academic audience. What kind of voice would be required for the correct reading aloud of the lines with which our discussion opened?

> Haste thee nymph, and bring with thee
> Jest and youthful Jollity,
> Quips and Cranks, and wanton Wiles,
> Nods, and Becks, and Wreathed Smiles . . .

The quick answer would be that the lines should be read elegantly and neatly in a 'light' voice. Why? Because such a voice in such a manner is appropriate to the mood and the subject. But this could be only an approximate prescription—approximate because it could be used equally well to suggest the correct manner for reading aloud, say, Thomas Hood's *Plea of the Midsummer Fairies*. And at once we realize that the prescription fails and that what is only approximate must be false. There were no fairies at the bottom of Milton's garden (he regretted their departure, the departure of 'the yellow-skirted *Fayes*'); but Hood, whom the fairies had never approached, pretended that he believed them, and asked his readers to join in the game of 'let's pretend'. The prescription does no justice to the coolness of Milton's tone (the coolness required for the saying of Milton), a coolness and crispness inherent in the formality of his poetry. This formality pre-supposes a detachment between Milton and his material; and we are here mindful of a key phrase in the commentary of Brooks and Hardy, namely 'Milton tends to employ, from the very beginning, a large measure of aesthetic distance'.[1] That distance, the formality consequent on that distance, demands a certain sharpness in the physical utterance of Milton's lines; the poem is to ring clearly and cleanly. Hood's poem, on the contrary, like other poems of the nineteenth century which ask of readers or listeners to temporarily *lend* a belief (which they do not own) requires for its reading aloud a warm, hazy and coaxing tone. Nineteenth-century fairy poems, even *The Eve of St Agnes*, are to be emotionally believed in by the auditors for the duration of the spell, the spell being ob-

---

[1] In *Poems of Mr John Milton:* the 1645 Edition. Ed. C. Brooks and J. E. Hardy, New York, 1951.

tained by a vocal blur[1] to the edge of the words, by the use of tremulo. But Milton's lines are to be said—were said—with precision, not only because of this 'distance' or 'formality' but also because of the nature and size of an actual or actually supposed audience. *L'Allegro*, if Tillyard is right, and all the tokens go to show that he is, was conceived as being delivered before an actual audience, a semi-public audience of some size assembled for an academic occasion. By contrast, Hood was writing for a hoped-for audience of, at best, a few friends, assembled in the study of the author or in the drawing-room of someone who had bought and liked his poems and who, with luck, might ask or—if he politely demurred—entreat, him to recite. This audience must have existed almost always in hope only. Tennyson's audience was of the same order, but there was this difference: he would summon his private audience rather than be summoned by it, and for this summoned audience he composed aloud in the terms of his own voice.[2]

That Milton was practised at addressing an audience aloud during the period in which he composed *l'Allegro* is attested by the Latin *Prolusions*. Tillyard especially marks the close connection between *l'Allegro–Il Penseroso* and the First Prolusion namely, 'Whether Day or Night is the more excellent'. The vocal delivery of these exercises would have attuned Milton's ear to the acoustic conditions of a particular hall and accustomed him to the expectancies of a particular audience; and a respect, acquired by experience, for both auditorium and audience would have counted with a poet who came to compose nothing—for his prose cannot be excepted—but that which he imagined as being sounded aloud. All he composed he therefore tested against the capacities of his own vocal organs, actually or memorially.

As for that Cambridge audience, for which *l'Allegro* was designed as a construction in sound, it was nothing if not critical. It would have regarded Euphrosyne, Zephir and Aurora with

---

[1] 'Fur' instead of 'blur'—a tactile not an auditory metaphor—might be better. In attempting to describe tone we seem inexorably bound to metaphor. All nineteenth-century poets are furry—Keats has fur, Hood has fur, Tennyson has most fur, but Milton has no fur. A main effort of the twentieth-century poets has been to get rid of the fur and to attain once more an incisive voice.

[2] *Vide supra*, pp. 55–56.

the same detachment as the poet. It would have set these pagan
nymphs and deities within the same frame of interested dis-
belief. Not only would it have beheld the nymphs and deities
at the same 'aesthetic distance', but it would have been equally
conscious of doing so. So the words

> Haste thee nymph, and bring with thee . . .

must be carved in air, clearly and blithely. In Milton's 'tuneable voice'—if, as we argue, he conceived his poetry in terms
of that instrument—the high-pitched ring of the line had a
keen and hard edge. The timbre of Milton's voice, at this stage
of his life not yet harsh, is exquisitely sharp. The lines must be
said with the right tang. There is no comma before 'nymph'
and none, either grammatical or rhetorical, should be inserted when the poem is recreated in sound, for there should be
no 'romantic' pause and drop of the voice before mention of the
mythological. There should be no need to ask of the audience a
'let's pretend' act. On the contrary, Euphrosyne *hastes* into the
picture bringing with her 'Jest and youthful Jollity'.

After the neat and well-defined pause at the end of the first
line (notice how the second 'thee'[1] in *Haste thee nymph, and
bring with thee* is longer than the first), there is a rise in pitch and
an increased force of utterance in 'Jest'.[2] The passage we quote
begins on a high and strong note in 'Haste'—high because of
the sound [ei], and yet higher because the sound occurs in an
Imperative. (The pitch of a vowel in a verb is modified by the
grammatical form assumed by that verb. 'Haste' as an Imperative is higher than 'haste' in the Indicative 'we haste'.) Indeed,
each of the other three lines in the passage we have quoted is
marked either by a rise in pitch or an access of force—on 'Jest',
'Quips' and 'Nods' respectively. The punctuation shows

---

[1] Longer because it occurs at the end of a line; also, because of its two
preceding vowels. So that the series reads i, i, iː (whereas the sequence of
the first hemistich is ei, i, iː). Because the vowel of the second 'thee' is longer,
its 'th-' [ð] has to be more strongly stressed in proportion.

[2] Naturally because, whatever the metre, pitch tends to drop at the end of
a line. In iambics the first syllable is almost always an anacrusis—a mounting block for the recovery of pitch at the head of *its* line which, in turn, will
have declined by the time of its conclusion. In trochaics, as here, the
'block' is dispensed with and the mount is leapt from the ground.

whether this access is to be of pitch, or of force, or of both.
Thus the absence of a comma after 'Quips' in

> Quips and Cranks, and wanton Wiles

distinguishes the proper sounding of that line from its successor

> Nods, and Becks, and Wreathed Smiles.

The former line, because the vowels of its first three syllables
are on a descending scale, requires no pause; the latter, because
the first three syllables employ an ascending scale, requires a
pause before the vocal change of gear demanded by the high
'Becks'. Milton prevents his poem from degenerating by his
determination that the opening sound of each line shall be
keyed-up. Thus one could quote other examples where the
first sound of a line boosts declining energy or maintains and
ensures the general high pitch of the whole:

> While the Plowman neer at hand
> *Whistles* ore the Furrow'd Land . . .
>
> (63–64)

or

> Oft list'ning how the Hounds and horn,
> *Chearly* rouse the slumb'ring morn . . .
>
> (54–55)

—each illustrative of a device by which the general pitch (and
so spirit or temper) of the poem is sustained.

Without possessing a gramophone record of the first performance of *l'Allegro* we can hear the voice for which, and
through which, it was composed.

Certainly that voice was 'tuneable', but clear and defined,
with a hard tang to it, even when it essayed something approaching what Dr Johnson termed 'levity' though, I dare say,
Dr Johnson was even more ill-equipped by disposition—and
voice—to essay 'levity' than Milton! Yet, to be just, Dr Johnson
finds little levity in *l'Allegro* and not much 'asperity' in *Il
Penseroso*. To Dr Johnson the companion poems were 'two noble
efforts of imagination' but did not appear to be sufficiently
opposite in sound or effect. Against this judgment, Mr Brooks
and Mr Hardy note that Milton had not been concerned to
exploit 'mere contrast'. Rather, they say: 'By choosing the
obvious contrast between mirth and melancholy, Milton

obligated himself to bring them as close together as possible in their effect on the mind.'[1] In fact, as far as voice is concerned, the kind of voice Milton required, or which any voice would require, to read them aloud effectively (which is accurately) needs no control over contrast. The voice needed for *l'Allegro* must not be, either in tone or expression, thin, soft or frivolous; and the voice needed for *Il Penseroso* must not be hollow or sepulchral, nor yet resonant. It too must be carved neatly in air. That conceded, it is true that, though the metre is the same, the tempo of *Il Penseroso* is slightly, but perceptibly, slower:

> Or let my Lamp at midnight hour,
> Be seen in som high lonely Towr,
> Where I may oft out-watch the *Bear:*
> With thrice great *Hermes*, or unsphear
> The spirit of Plato to unfold. . . .

Here there is no sudden bracing up of the pitch at the head of each line—such as we found in *l'Allegro*—because the first syllable is unstressed and is lower in the natural scale than the stressed syllable which follows it; besides which the slightly slower tempo demands a slightly lower pitch. Nevertheless the voice, as in *l'Allegro*, is still clear and plangent with just a touch of that *harshness* which, more than any other single quality, is what struck Dr Johnson most in his consideration of the poetry of Milton. But it is suggested here that what struck Dr Johnson so forcibly as 'harsh' was not, or not merely, or even primarily, Milton's severity of puritanical or republican opinions, but a harshness of physical voice expressive perhaps of a temperament disposed to adopt such opinions. This touch of harshness, or tendency towards harshness, is not only properly found when Milton is saying harsh things (when the meaning is married to the sense), but is present when the meaning is void of harshness. Phonologically, it results from Milton's inclination to use—apart from the *littera canina*—two sounds, the alveolar nasal n [n] and the velar nasal -ng [ŋ] with a quite peculiar frequency. No other poet in English uses these two sounds so habitually, so pervasively as Milton. Whenever anyone is expressing anger they tend to occur often. Milton uses them often when he is not angry, and their presence then is a main

[1] *Vide supra*, p. 134.

contribution to his vocal tang or hardness, its individual timbre. He is however often angry, perhaps because of his partiality towards these sounds and the effectiveness with which he could use them, and then we have something like this famous passage (the nasals are here italicized):

> Two massy Keyes he bore of metals twai*n*,
> (The Golde*n* opes, the Iro*n* shuts amai*n*)
> He shook his Miter'd locks, and ster*n* bespake,
> How well could I have spar'd for thee young swai*n*,
> A*n*ow of such as for their bellies sake,
> Creep and i*n*trude, and climb i*n*to the fold?
> Of other care they little reck'*n*ing make,
> The*n* how to scramble at the shearers feast,
> And shove away the worthy bidde*n* guest;
> Bli*n*d mouthes! that scarce themselves k*n*ow how to hold
> A Sheep-hook, or have lear*n*'d ought els the least
> That to the faithful Herdma*n*s art belo*n*gs!
> And whe*n* they list, their lea*n* and flashy so*n*gs
> Grate on their scra*nn*el Pipes of wretched straw,
> The hu*n*gry Sheep look up, and are *n*ot fed,
> But swol*n* with wi*n*d, a*n*d the ra*n*k mist they draw,
> Rot i*n*wardly, and foul co*n*tagio*n* spread:
> Besides what the gri*m* Woolf with privy paw
> Daily devours apace, and *n*othi*n*g sed,
> But that two-ha*n*ded e*n*gine at the door,
> Sta*n*ds ready to smite o*n*ce, and smite *n*o more.
>   (*Lycidas*, II, 110–131)

Lycidas (1637) ends the early career. Or it is middle Milton, since, while concluding the series of earlier poems, it shows a Milton committed to sectarian-religious and party-political interests. Those interests led to the series of prose pamphlets, and consequently to the almost total suspension of his poetry for many years. Anger, indignation and scorn—the same passions as burst out in *Lycidas*—animate the pamphlets and are vocally, literally vocally, expressed.[1] Now it might be said that the

---

[1] A parallel from the prose:
I have something also to the Divines, the brief to what were needful, not to be Disturbers of the Civil Affairs, being in hands better able, and to whom it more belongs to manage them; but to study harder, and to attend the Office of good Pastors, not perform'd by mounting twice into the Chair with a formal Preachment huddl'd up at the odd hours of a whole lazy Week, but by incessant pains and watching—which if they well consider'd, how little leisure would they find

passage from that poem is peculiarly suitable to the present argument and was therefore chosen to illustrate Milton's use of n [n] and -ng [ŋ] in a harsh, heady and nasalized anger (and let us remember, when we come to the line 'Grate on their scrannel Pipes of wretched straw,'[1] that, additionally, Milton sounded the R 'very hard'.) Yet an exceptional frequency of these strong, harsh and heady n and -ng sounds is not confined to pure invective. They occur just as remarkably in the very early *On the Morning of Christ's Nativity*, in such stanzas as:

> With such a horrid clang
> As on mount *Sinai* rang
> > While the red fire, and smouldring clouds out brake:
> The aged Earth agast
> With terrour of that blast,
> > Shall from the surface to the center shake;
> When at the worlds last session,
> The dreadful Judge in middle Air shall spread his throne.
>
> (XVII)

or

> *Peor*, and *Baalim*,
> Forsake their Temples dim,
> > With twice batter'd god of *Palestine*,
> And mooned Ashtaroth,

---

to be the most pragmatical Sidesmen of every popular Tumult and Sedition? And all this while they are to learn what the true end and reason is of the Gospel which they teach, and what a world it differs from the censorious and supercilious lording over Conscience. It would be good also they liv'd so as might persuade the People they hated Covetousness, which, worse than Heresy, is Idolatry; hated Pluralities and all kind of Simony; left rambling from Benefice to Benefice, like ravenous Wolves, seeking where they may devour the biggest. Let them be sorry that, being cal'd to assemble about reforming the Church, they fell to progging and solliciting the Parlament (tho they had renounc'd the name of Priests) for a new settling of their Tithes and Oblations and doublelin'd themselves with spiritual places of Commodity beyond the possible discharge of their Duty. Let them assemble in Consistory with their Elders and Deacons to the preserving of Church-Disciplin each in his several charge, and not a pack of Clergymen by themselves to bellychear in their presumptuous *Sion*. . . .

Tenure of Kings and Magistrats (1649)

[1] 'Their' not 'thir'—the strong dysyllabic form of the possessive.

That Milton is the great poet of anger was remarked long ago by Aldous Huxley in *Texts and Pretexts*. A full recognition of this aspect of Milton is to be found, as the title indicates, in G. Wilson Knight's *Chariot of Wrath* (Faber & Faber, 1942).

Heav'ns Queen and Mother both,
   Now sits not girt with Tapers holy shine,
The Libye *Hammon* shrinks his horn,
In vain the *Tyrian* Maids their wounded Thammuz mourn.

And sullen *Moloch* fled,
Hath left in shadows dred,
   His burning Idol all of blackest hue,
In vain with Cymbals ring,
They call the grisly king,
   In dismall dance about the furnace blue,
The brutish gods of *Nile* as fast,
Isis and *Orus*, and the Dog *Anubis* hast.

                (XXII–XXIII)

The hard, polished, the 'marmoreal', surface of Milton's
poetry has often been alluded to, and that surface has been a
ground of critical attack on his reputation. But it should be
realized that Milton conceived his poems as objects for performance, and for performance by his own physical voice. Milton, in composing, heard them *as if they were being sounded aloud
by his own voice*. He therefore wrote within the bounds of his own
voice and concentrated on what his own voice could most
effectively utter. We can deduce that voice from the printed
signs which record it. In his earlier years, though it was 'tuneable'—i.e. expertly controlled by a musical intelligence—it was
also sharp and plangent. The early poems, the musical structures
which his voice developed, for all their beautiful clarity of a
lifted pitch (demanded by the kind of actual or envisaged audience), have an individual timbre which is harsh but pleasing.
The possession of this instrument, this voice, probably determined Milton's detachment from his matter, ensured that
'large measure of aesthetic distance'; it probably (though
whether temperament more conditioned voice, or voice temperament is impossible to say: we *can* say that they matched)
also increasingly disposed him to themes and subjects which
could often invoke his anger, scorn and indignation. But even
in poems exquisitely innocent of rancour, such as the songs *To
Echo* and 'Sabrina Fair' in *Comus* (which, as a whole, must be
regarded somewhat differently—as a *dramatic* poem, a poem in
which Milton attempts to speak through voices other than his
own, which he probably expressly designed for the voices of

Lawes and the Egerton children), there is a hard, polished lucidity attributable in some degree to the qualities of the voice which conceived and made them.

Later, Milton's voice dropped in pitch, and he exploited the possibilities of resonance which this drop offered.

iii

It is our proposition that Milton's voice, like any other man's voice, changed in the course of years. It is not our intention to trace this change, stage by stage, by an analysis of the occasional sonnets composed between *Lycidas* and *Paradise Lost*. That could hardly be done even if it were worth while. It could hardly be done because the process of change taking place day by day, year by year, though certain is imperceptible. What applies to Milton applies to all men. If we hear a man, after an absence of twenty years, we recognize a vocal change (as well as the vocal identity); if we hear him at day to day intervals, we do not. Further, no voice, though every voice changes with the years, changes consistently. A man, whether he is a poet or not —but this can be discerned in the work of poets where printed marks betoken sounds—can anticipate, according to state of health or his mood, the voice he is to habitually use twenty years hence; equally, a middle-aged man, when plaintive and self-pitiful, say, can unconsciously resort to the tones and shriller accents he had habitually used twenty years in the past. Further, it would be unprofitable, if not impossible, to trace the from day to day changes in the voice of Milton for this reason: Milton, no less than all other self-possessed men, whatever the degree of their self-possession (and Milton was highly self-possessed[1]), sometimes liked to—had to—aimed to—speak in (or through) the *per*sons of others not himself. The slightest practice at self-observation or observation of others will confirm this. Yet, when this allowance is taken into account, it will be conceded that Milton was more of an *egotistical sublime* than most, and was therefore the less ready either to be possessed by, or to invade, the voices of identities not his. *Egotistical sublime* is,

[1] 'Self-possessed'—another instance where one is reduced to (what can only be) a metaphor to signify what one means with any sort of tolerable accuracy.

of course, the phrase employed by Keats of Wordsworth. But Keats' implicit (though no *explicit* declaration, compelled by Keats' temperament, could be so taut or damaging) 'nailing' of the post-1807 Wordsworth applies to Milton no less. Milton, an intractable and exceedingly masculine egoist—despite that early 'Lady of Christ's' eulogium—was more unable and unwilling to speak in the persons of others than most. What is practicable and important (if only because the years between 1637 and 1658 were extraordinarily lean or sparse in the case of Milton whereas, in the case of Shakespeare, the middle stretch of life was far otherwise) is, rather, the difference in the voice of the poet which composed the *Nativity Ode* or *l'Allegro* and the voice (after the long break given over to polemics) of the poet of *Paradise Lost*.

The voice of *Paradise Lost*, measured against the voice of the early poems, has deepened a great deal. His temperament has become graver, so has his vocal organ. That drop, expressive or not of political disappointment, events in his private life, the ineluctable darkening of hope (against original inclinations of temperament) over the intervening years, is a—almost *the*—condition for the existence of *Paradise Lost*.

To quote some lines from that poem:

> Farr / in th' Horizon // to the North / appear'd //
> From skirt to skirt / a fierie Region, // stretcht //
> In battailous aspect // and / neerer view //
> Bristl'd // with upright beams / innumerable
> Of rigid Spears // and Helmets throng'd // and Shields //
> Various, // with boastful Argument / portraid, //
> The banded Powers of *Satan* / hasting on /
> With furious expedition . . .
>
> (VI, 78–86)

—a passage which has been the subject of some brilliant comment by Sergei Eisenstein.[1] The signs / or //, which have been inserted, indicate the pauses which, according to the interpretation now being advanced, must be followed if the lines are to sound as Milton heard and sounded them. This

---

[1] Eisenstein, the film-producer, in *The Film Sense* (Faber, 1943), pp. 54–58. Most Miltonists, and most students of literature, presumably because of the unlikelihood suggested by the title, are ignorant of the comment to which I refer.

does not mean that the pause // is exactly twice as long as the pause /. Probably no two pauses indicated // are of exactly equal duration value, and no two pauses indicated / are of exactly equal duration value. What is meant is that the sign // indicates a pause that is appreciably longer than the pause /; but that the pause /, the shorter of the two—though it is of no standard length—is yet generally more pronounced (of longer duration) than most either silent or non-silent modern readers of Milton pretend.

If this last assertion were disputed, the reply would be based partly on reference to acoustics; partly on a reference to the increased tempo of spoken—and so also poetic—English since 1660; partly on a reference to what yet once more must be called the 'Epic Tradition'.[1] The first and third of these were within Milton's knowledge. We must combine these with *his* knowledge of the natural change in his voice (which had taken place since the period of his early poems and which was also sufficiently real to himself) to explain the achievement between 1658 and 1663 when he dictated *Paradise Lost*.

To take the second and most important area of reference (that relating to the increased tempo of spoken—and so poetic—English) first: something of which Milton, necessarily lacking a foresight of processes that were to continue over the three centuries after his death, was unconscious.

Crudely put (since this is but a *resumé* of common knowledge), the tempo of English speech since the age of Milton and Bunyan has increased. Certainly there are all manner of situations in modern life where words are uttered slowly, but here we are summarizing a general truth. The rate of acceleration varied according to place and time. The generations overlap; moreover, some individuals were robustly conservative in their speech, others were progressive—though 'progressive' is hardly the word since progress denotes gain, and the change we are alluding to, if it involved gain, also involved loss—perhaps a loss more considerable than gain. Bunyan, for example, though living and writing into the late, i.e. post-Restoration, seventeenth century, sounds antediluvian beside Congreve, as much because of his slow tempo as because of his old-world religious and moral seriousness. But Bunyan's seriousness and his tempo

[1] See C. M. Bowra: *From Virgil to Milton* (Macmillan, 1945).

went together and, by contrast, the restored Court, in putting a premium on brilliant and witty chatter, discouraged conversation relating to those areas of emotion and thought which require a slow utterance. Conversation, if it is to be brilliant and witty, needs to be rapid, and Congreve's dialogue set a standard for conversation among all those with a claim to fashion, rank and politeness. Writers were among those with such a claim, and Pope's poetry has something about it of *vers de societé*.

Such remarks would obscure rather than illuminate if they were taken as the sole explanation of the change in tempo to which we are referring. The existence, after the Restoration, of an urban caste or class, with a conscious striving after elegance and fashion, was only one of a whole complex of mutually operating causes (linguistic, psychological, economic, social, political) which created a change in the tempo of English speech and English writing—a tempo which distinguishes the Authorized Version, the Book of Common Prayer, Milton or Bunyan, on the one hand, from Dryden, Congreve, Addison or Pope on the other. But of these causes one deserves particular mention.

The rapid spread, in the later seventeenth and early eighteenth centuries, of the ability to read silently radically effected the pace of written and spoken English. During this period the modern habit, where the eye merely follows printed signs on the page, and comprehends those signs as meanings, without first—as a necessary and intermediary act—converting them into a series of sounds became sufficiently widespread to effect the tempo of verse. People began to speak, or to suppose they spoke, at the rate at which they apprehended mute signs and, by 'people' is meant precisely that caste or class whose interest in literature, fashion and politics was proprietorial.

But Milton cannot be read aloud at the pace at which we have become accustomed to read silently; and to read him silently at the pace at which we normally read silently is to destroy him. To say the lines of Milton more rapidly than the pace he heard and designed them is to raise the pitch—and the pitch of *Paradise Lost* is part of the meaning. It is also to reduce the silences during which so much happens, or ought to happen. For it must be admitted that when language is spoken above a certain rate individual words can lose semantic richness; they are not allowed time for the release of their various levels of

meaning or of their associations on one level.[1] The tempo of
Paradise Lost is slower than that of the early poems, and is a
property of Milton's later voice. The pace is not solely regulated
by the pauses // or / any more than it is solely by the length of
the vowels or consonantal combinations. The one requires, and
is dependent on, the other, and both are consequent on acoustics
and on Milton's conviction that an epic ought to be sublime.[2]

The acoustics.—It may seem difficult to deduce the shape and
size of hall Milton assumed for *Paradise Lost*. Not that we suppose Milton ever confidently *expected* the realization in sound of
his epic in an actual hall, but yet he imagined one. He *imagined*
an auditorium the size and shape of which were best fitted for
the saying and hearing of his poem; and the way Milton wished
it to be said—his own way—is declared by the printed signs.
As the Early Poems were either composed for actual audiences,
seated in an actual auditorium, or composed on that pre-
supposition, so does *Paradise Lost* presuppose (or imagine) an
actual hall and an audience of 'fit though few', even if the *ideal*
(which the actual must *point to*) auditorium for *Paradise Lost* was
infinite and its audience all mankind.[3]

Now the pauses, those medial, or terminal, creative silences,
indicated in the passage quoted from Book VI (see p. 103
above) are an acoustical necessity—granting the special kind of
voice assumed, and required, by the poetry with its 'sense variously drawn out from one Verse into another'. A pause or
suspension at the end of each line is acoustically required for a
sufficient absorption—or dying away—of the resonance generated. Without such a pause, the opening sounds of the following

[1] Though this depends on the pace of receptivity an author has managed
to work up in his audience or readers. As the excitement of suspense in-
creases so does the pace of receptivity, but Milton chose a fable in which
there could be no suspense—the outcome of each situation being only too
well-known in advance.

[2] Despite what has been said of an increase in the general rate of spoken
English, obviously something of the Miltonic tempo, thanks to Thomson
and other eighteenth-century imitators, survived to the time of Wordsworth
and beyond. A tempo that was originally determined (at least partly) by
Milton's physical organs of speech became in time a mark of the Grand
Style whether or no the *writer* was equal to its utterance.

[3] *Paradise Regained* presupposes a lighter and quicker delivery, a smaller
audience and a smaller and non-reverberative auditorium.

line or half-line would be 'drowned' or blurred. But what is required by acoustics is also required semantically: during the
silence the listeners are left to ponder the associations roused or
speculate their own continuation of a sense which has been
suspended. The function of the Miltonic pause or 'cliff-hanger'
has been the subject of a good deal of comment before but not, I
think, with the exact sort of aim intended here.[1] Thus a further
illustration is justified:

(1)   At last //
(2) Farr / in th' Horizon // to the North / appeer'd /
(3) From skirt to skirt/ a fierie Region, // stretcht
(4) In battailous aspect. . . .

To recall the situation: A vast multitude of rebellious angels
is advancing in military formation on the throne of God. The
point of view, the physical viewpoint, now switches to that of the
defence, the loyalists. The loyal battalions, drawn up in expectation, perceive a menacing glow on the horizon. Now how
are we asked to hear the lines being said?

After (1) 'at last' [æt + laɪst] (the vowel of 'last' is very long,
almost disyllabic, beginning deep-pitched it rises slightly in
scale to terminate in the forward sibilant and following plosive)
there is a pause //. During that pause the resonance generated
by the aɪ diminishes and dies away. (The longer the vowel, the
more forcefully it is sounded, the lower its tonic pitch the greater
the resonance generated and the longer the pause needed for
its absorption.) But during that pause, while the resonance dies
away, each member of the audience—and this applies to each
reader if he is hearing Milton's voice and not simply perusing
the lines with his eyes—is creating for himself his own object of
expectancy; or he intensifies his expectancy—'at last . . .
what?' But the satisfaction of his curiosity is to be delayed as it
was for the watchers on the 'Chrystall wall'.

(2) Farr / in th' Horizon // to the North / appeer'd /

The R in 'Farr' is doubled, and Milton sounded his R's
'very hard'. But any rolled final R necessitates, for physical

---

[1] Miltonic, but it is mainly restricted to *Paradise Lost*. Pauses are expected
at the end of each line of *Paradise Regained* (as at the end of every line
Milton wrote) but they are less weighty than in *Paradise Lost*, nor have
they the same purpose.

reasons, a stop for the renewal of breath. Thus the line begins not with a trochee (Fárr in): on the contrary, 'Farr' stands separately on the page. A long pause precedes, and a short pause, succeeds it. The double *littera canina* (the Miltonic snarl) forces the vowel in 'Farr' [aɪ] to adopt a pitch somewhat higher than the nominally identical vowel in 'last' and, because higher, it is inevitably shorter. Now the pause after 'Farr' (essential for the renewal of breath) results in two following dactylic feet:

in th' Horizon // to the North /

with the pitch rising and the pace quickening. If it is objected that the first of these feet is not dactylic (that it is not ◡ ◡ - but ◡ ◡ ◡ - ◡), one must reply that the third of these unstressed syllables is syncopated, and the final syllable in 'Horizon', [ən] is dissolved in the pause required by the high-pitched (but sharp and vibrant) ai in 'Horizon'.

Milton's voice, in what is now effectively two trisyllabic feet, rises towards two crests, but[1]

in th' Ho - ri - zon   to the North

---

[1] Key to Notation: LONG — — — — — — — SHORT

The notation here used is intended only to give a vague, not an exact, indication of pitch and time. Musical notation is too rigid to allow of any exact indication of speech rhythms and intonation. Thus ♪ is longer than ♩ and ♩ than ♪, but these are not related to the precise musical values normally associated with these notes. Similarly no clef has been inserted, since only the idea of comparative height and depth is here attempted.

is higher than , but not by an exact semitone. No time signature is given, as this would have little meaning in the present context. A rising or falling line after a note indicates a gradual rise or fall of pitch during that syllable.

In the preparation of this notation the author gratefully acknowledges the help of Dr Roger Bullivant.

with the pause after 'North', the word 'appeer'd' reduces, or brings down, the pitch to tonic in preparation for a particularly long span in the next line:

(3) From skirt to skirt / a fierie Region // stretcht

particularly long because the / after 'skirt' is less a breath inter-val than a 'catch' or minimal hiatus in the flow of sound, neces-sary merely for the strong charge to bridge the soar in 'fierie', which is certainly trisyllabic [ai ə i]; while also trisyllabic is 'Region'.

'Stretcht' what? or in what? There is the hover or suspension while listeners, or readers, surmise what they wish or will; and the word 'stretcht' is protracted, rising in scale, to suit the mean-ing, before the violent, high-pitched, but harsh and nearly shouted (each syllable short):

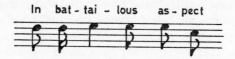

Then a long pause precedes, and a short pause succeeds 'and', before

followed, after the pause, by:

which leads to a line of three metrical feet uttered with extraordinary force:

Of   ri-gid speers   and hel-mets throng'd   and shields

ending with the largest of pauses while the audience speculate
on the nature of the 'Shields'.

Thus one is forced to do, what one had hoped to avoid: employ
a form of musical notation to demonstrate the movement of a
piece of Milton's verse while it is being sounded. We have tried
to show the way the passage ought to be said. Each element of
the printed text contributes to a passage of poetry, but it is only
poetry while it is actually being performed and heard, or when
such a performance is being remembered, or when an out-
wardly silent performance is created, in obedience to the signs
for sound, in imagination, for the enjoyment of the inner ear.
Otherwise, the passage is only a 'score', an aggregate of signs
or directions which, if followed, result in the experience called
poetry. Idiosyncratic spelling, punctuation, capitalization help to
define Milton's vocal identity in the composition of this passage.
The capitals in 'Spears', 'Helmets', 'Shields', for instance, indicate that these words should be sounded with particular force.

It is not, of course, being argued that the sound of Milton is
autonymous of the meaning or, still less, that it is at odds with
the meaning. It is true that Mr Eliot and Dr Leavis have made
the point, more or less explicitly, that the sound and the 'meaning' in Milton are not identical or organically fused; have
suggested that the intellectual and emotional rewards of the
'meaning' do not live up to the grandeur of the sound. This
charge seems unfounded because the 'meaning' can only appear
meagre or inadequate when the text is read by the eye alone
and at the rapid pace to which the eye is now accustomed.
When that happens the meaning is weighed by the intellect in
disengagement from the act of hearing. But, as we have realized, such a silent, such an eye-and-intellect-alone reading of
Milton is unjust, for the eye then proceeds at quite the wrong
tempo; it far outstrips the pace with which Milton is composing
with his voice, is not geared to that sound. Read aloud in Milton's voice, the meaning has an encasing grandeur of sound.

That encasement does not inflate the meaning, rather it produces the meaning intended.

The voice behind the lines we have discussed is the voice of Milton, the narrator. The narrator is the main person (literally person) of *Paradise Lost*, but there are other speakers: God the Father, Christ, Satan, Adam and Eve, etc. They are all magniloquent. Even when Adam is said to whisper, as in V. 17–26, the utterance is stately and orotund, for the truth is that when Milton concludes with a 'so Satan spake', or an 'He ended frowning', or a 'Thus Belial', or a 'This said, he sat', or a 'So promised hee', the speeches referred to, whether delivered by a person divine, angelic or human, though cast in the form of *oratio recta* are more actually *oratio obliqua*. What the characters said in their persons is being relayed through the medium of the narrator's voice. The poem is nowhere dramatic in the sense that the narratives of Chaucer became dramatic when the poet inhabits, or mimics, the voices of his speakers. What happens in the dialogue of Milton is that the characters inflect the voice of the narrator with tones agreeable to the moods and rôles the Fable obliges them to adopt. Such vocal variety as there is in *Paradise Lost* represents the extent of Milton's own voice in middle age.

What is called Milton's late style, in contrast to his early style, records a change of the physical voice. The voice deepened. No less than in the case of the early poems, its owner assumed himself to be delivering his epic aloud, and it is with that consciousness that he dictated the poem, insisting on spellings that as closely as possible recorded his own pronunciation and timbre.

After he had concluded *Paradise Lost*, did Milton's voice undergo further change? That it did is suggested by such lines from *Paradise Regained* as:

> This having heard, strait I again revolv'd
> The Law and Prophets, searching what was writ
> Concerning the Messiah . . .
>
> (I, 259–261)

> To whom quick answer Satan thus returnd.
> *Belial*, in much uneven scale thou weigh'st
> All others by thy self . . .
>
> (II, 172–174)

After a night of storm so ruinous,
Cleard up their choicest notes in bush and spray
To gratulate the sweet return of morn;

(IV, 436–438)

So talk'd he, while the Son of God went on
And staid not, but in brief him answerd thus.

(IV, 484–485)

As Tillyard points out, in *Paradise Regained* Milton was making a Little or Short Epic, a variety clearly differentiated in his own mind from the Full Length Epic. No doubt he conceived of himself as addressing a smaller audience in less echoic surroundings. Equally, he may have been concerned to experience what his voice could do in a minor key. However that may be, the verse—which is to say the voice—is moving (in comparison with the voice of *Paradise Lost*) more quickly and lightly. How do we know this? The answer is provided by the answer to the question: How ought *Paradise Regained* to be read aloud? In *Paradise Regained* the lengthy and deliberate pauses for the absorption of resonance disappear. The voice is tired and remote and exercising itself in surroundings less vast. Later still it was to seek, in *Samson Agonistes*, renewal of energy through the discovery of new rhythms. The new rhythms called out attributes of Milton's voice which otherwise would never have been heard.

Finally, since *Paradise Lost* and its successors were dictated (they are the only considerable poems we know of to have been dictated), they are exceptionally good examples to adduce in support of the theory that a poet's physical voice conditions his work, and that changes of voice cause changes in his 'style'. But it is important to realize that the theory must not be pushed too far. The evidence and arguments we have offered so far entitle us only to assert that in the case of *some* poets at least there is a demonstrably intimate relationship between their voices and their work—especially since in the case of these, if not of all poets, poetry was regarded as essentially a spoken form. To claim that changes of voice are causative of changes of what has been called 'style' might seem however too hazardous —even despite common experience which assures us that all men, if and when they change (in personality), change also their manner of speech. Many might urge that the change in personality is primary (and first in time), and that a change in voice and manner of speech is subsequently developed to express that change.

Too little is as yet known about such matters to allow us to be dogmatic one way or the other. Besides, in the case of one man the change in personality might come first, in another the vocal change might come first, and in a third the changes might occur simultaneously. Further, poets, whose trade is vocal sound, ought perhaps to be regarded as belonging to a special category in this one respect. Further, again, poets differ among themselves, but it is just to consider Milton—more than many others —as unusually concerned with sound, especially speech-sound, even among poets.

Too little is known. We said that 'Milton's late style, in contrast to his early style, records a change of the physical voice. The voice deepened' (the first statement is a fact, the second and third statements are postulates in explanation of that fact— postulates based on how we *ought* and *do* hear the poem while we 'read' it). It might be urged that the vocal change was either a concomitant or a consequence of the change of style (and of personality) rather than a cause. That may or may not be the case, but we can at least be sure that whether or no the vocal change occurred earlier than that change in personality (or whether both were expressive of that factor X to which we referred earlier), yet, once established, the relationship between voice and mind was one of continual interaction, one of mutual influence—one or the other being generally dominant.

PART THREE

POETIC DRAMATIST AND DRAMATIC POET

VII Shakespeare's Voice and the Voices of His Instruments

i

So far we have considered poets who spoke in their own persons: Tennyson, Shelley, Milton. Or if these did not professedly speak for themselves, they yet used their own voices to speak for others—a dying swan, a skylark, God.

It is time now to consider a dramatic poet, a poet whose main work consists of lines intended to be delivered aloud not by himself but by people, men and boys, whom he knew (and, in the result, by others whom he did not know—by actors and actresses of many generations down to today).

Yet it might be urged, for the purposes of the contrast that we aim to establish (namely, that between the poet who professedly speaks in his own person and the poet who speaks in—or through—the persons of others), that we could have selected Chaucer; that the great narrative poet, no less than the great dramatic poet, wrote words intended to be uttered through throats other than his own. But there is a difference: Chaucer composed, as far as we know, for himself as an actor, not for others as actors. Chaucer's own voice, when he read aloud to his audience, contained or included the differing voices of the Prioress, the Monk, the Miller, etc. Inflecting his own voice, he would mimic the voices of his creatures. In quoting, say, the 'opinioun' of the Monk he would 'put on' the Monk's manner (if the Monk's manner might be a manner of bearing, there would certainly be a vocal manner to go with that bearing) of voice. Yet Chaucer does not 'put on' the Monk's vocal manner so completely as to deceive his hearers into thinking that he is doing more than imitate or mimic. If Chaucer had become the Monk, had ceased to contain the quoted voice of the Monk within his own, he would have ceased to be a great narrative poet and become something else.

Thus:

> And I seyde his opinioun was good,
> *What sholde he studie and make hymselven wood,*
> *Upon a book in cloystre alwey to poure,*
> *Or swynken with his handes, and laboure,*
> *As Austyn bit? How shal the world be served?*
> *Lat Austyn have his swynk to hym reserved!*
> Therefore he was a pricasour aright:
> Grehoundes he hadde as swift . . .[1]

The Monk's voice comes through as an echo. It is imitated by Chaucer in the lines I have italicized. But that it is imitation and not identification the pronoun shows. If it were identification we would have had not 'he studie' but 'I studie'. Chaucer's voice, then, for the space of the italicized lines, contained the Monk's voice—or the mannerisms and timbre of the Monk's voice are superimposed on Chaucer's.

But with Shakespeare it is far otherwise.

Except in his non-dramatic work, Shakespeare wrote lines cast in the First Person Singular, not for himself but for other men to sound aloud. He knew some of those men long and—it is a fair inference—intimately. In the course of years he came to appreciate or know the capacities and unique qualities of the voices of those men as well as—or better—than his own. Again this is a fair inference, since it was his business to appreciate or know them.

In this one yet vital respect of knowing thoroughly well the vocal powers of those men who were going to speak his lines, he was better positioned, or at any rate differently positioned, than his contemporaries. Unlike Shakespeare, Marlowe, Greene, Peele, Jonson, Webster, Beaumont and Fletcher were free-lances, they were not members of companies of Players.[2]

---

[1] General Prologue I (A), 183–190, ed. F. N. Robinson, O.U.P.

[2] Lyly, like Shakespeare, wrote for a single company, in his case the 'Boyes of Paules'. But boys have short lives as actors, four or five years at most.

Possibly a successful production of, say, *The Maid's Tragedy* led to the King's Men having (to use a publisher's term) an option on the author's next two scripts. Possibly. But whether this were so or not, the major dramatists, apart from Shakespeare, were not life-long shareholding members of those societies whose business it was to select and present plays for profit.[1] But Shakespeare was a member of a company of Players and became in time an important member with all the interest, security and responsibility attending his status as a shareholder. In that capacity, though he did some acting, especially in the earlier stages of his career, he gradually became chiefly useful as a purveyor of the scripts. At first he probably adapted or revised the scripts of others, making them more stageworthy in the light of his experience as an actor. More especially he revised in the light of his knowledge of the resources of the company to which he belonged. From thence he advanced to the composition of plays *ab initio*—but here again, and now more clearly, in the light of the resources of the company to which he belonged.

So much is commonly accepted but yet it has not been perhaps sufficiently borne in mind in every account of Shakespeare's growth as a poet, or in every consideration of those qualities of his work which distinguish it from the work of other poets, even from other Elizabethan and Jacobean dramatic poets.

Of whom did this particular company consist? In Shakespeare's company, of which he never became the chairman or first of the company directors, there was a proportion of hired casual labour—journeymen actors who, since they were employed 'by the day' only, came and went. Then there were the apprentices. These were boys who played women's parts until their voices broke.[2] These boys, who finished up as men, served seven years and, in their spare time, were servants or fags to some of the permanent senior members.

The voices of these boys and their personalities would change rapidly during their few years of adolescence. Like Lyly's players, their stage career was short, yet a few of them, their apprenticeships served, might remain on in the company as

---

[1] Jonson, for a while, was a hired or journeyman actor, though not, it seems, a very successful one.

[2] Though Solomon Pavy, who played old men, must not be forgotten.

adult actors and prosper. During those few years, while they were boys, their voices and personalities may have deeply impressed, not only audiences, but Shakespeare, both as poet and man.

But far more significant than the first group (the hired journeymen) and even—though only in the long run—more significant than the second, was the group of permanent members of the company, some of them also being shareholders, who formed the mainstay of each players' cast list year after year. We all know their names—Heminge, Cundell, Phillips, Burbage, etc.—and E. K. Chambers has mustered all the facts so far discovered relating to them.[1] During Shakespeare's active career in the company there were, in this class, some important retirements and deaths and some important recruits (for instance, Armin succeeded Kempe as principal comedian) but this holds: it was for the delivery by the voices of these permanent members—this inner set—that Shakespeare composed the bulk of his poetry. These were truly his 'fellows'. They were his instruments and he came to appreciate and exploit their contrasting capabilities and limitations. No two of these instruments were identical and not one remained unchanged. As Shakespeare's own voice changed with the years so did the voices of his instruments.

They were his instruments. Shakespeare actively used surrogates, or instruments. Unlike Shelley or Milton, he did not, it might seem, compose for his own voice as the agent except in his non-dramatic work—conspicuously in the *Sonnets*. In the *Sonnets* indeed, Shakespeare, like the other poets of whom we have treated, is an 'I' poet—more certainly so than in his narrative poems where frequently, in the manner of Chaucer, he echoes or imitates, or attempts to do so (inflecting or altering his own voice in the process), the voices of Venus, of Adonis, of Tarquin, of Lucrece.

The *Sonnets* were written over a period of years. Exactly how long that period was has not been decided and it is hard to see how it can ever be decided. W can only say that the latest possible date for their completion was 1609 when the Quarto was published. But relying on the internal evidence, on what is called stylistic change or development (but which really

[1] In *The Elizabethan Stage*, Vol. II (O.U.P., 1923).

signifies printed evidence of a change or development of personal voice), and on scraps of external evidence, and on a host of circumstantial probabilities, we can certainly say that the period for the composition of the *Sonnets* began somewhere between 1588–1593 and ended somewhere between 1603–1609.[1] The *Sonnets* were conceived and composed in terms of Shakespeare's own voice over a span of time ranging from between ten to nearly twenty years. During that span Shakespeare's physical voice changed for, even accepting the shorter period, a man's voice will have changed after ten years. The evidence, as we have said, is in the so-called 'stylistic development' of the *Sonnets*. But colaterally during that span he wrote a series of plays to be spoken on the stage by others. The composition of those plays, according as to whether we take the earlier or later limits for the 'sonnet' period, extends from—say—*The Two Gentlemen of Verona* (or *Love's Labour's Lost*) to 2 *Henry IV* (or *Hamlet* or *Measure for Measure*). These plays also, of course, show a development, a development at once poetic and dramatic. That development is parallel to the development of the *Sonnets*.

But, since the voices of Shakespeare's actors changed with the years hardly, or no, less than did Shakespeare's, the intention here is to indicate both the changes in Shakespeare's own voice and the changes in the voices of at least some of his instruments, and to suggest a relation between the two.

The kind of questions that arise are such as these: Did writing for voices outside himself—especially for one (probably Burbage's)—enable Shakespeare, as a poet, to go beyond himself? to orally convey by means of his surrogates areas of experience which otherwise (if he had limited himself simply to his own vocal resources) he could not have conveyed, and possibly

---

[1] L. Hotson in *Shakespeare's Sonnets Dated* argues an earliness for the composition of the whole sequence on grounds that few are able to accept. For instance, he says that the line in Sonnet 63 'The mortal moon hath her eclipse endured' refers to the crescent formation of the Armada as it was sighted in the Channel, and that therefore the Sonnet was written in 1588 or, soon after, in 1589. Even if the line does refer to the Armada rather than to the Queen's climacteric (which latter interpretation accords with Elizabethan mythology) there was nothing to prevent Shakespeare remembering the event of the Armada ten or twelve years after it had occurred.

The present writer favours *c.* 1592–*c.* 1603–4 as the period during which the *Sonnets* were written.

could not therefore have conceived? If so, did this distension, by employing the vocal instruments of others, cause him to abandon after 1603 (or by whatever year the sequence of *Sonnets* was concluded) compositions which he conceived of in terms of delivery through his own voice? Can we discern or re-hear the vocal history of one or more of these surrogates behind the printed signs on the pages—the pages of the earliest printed texts with all their peculiarities of punctuation, lineation, spelling, capitalization? The subject must be treated elliptically and cursorily for the subject deserves a book to itself.

ii

To start with Shakespeare as an 'I' poet writing the *Sonnets* which he conceived as being uttered aloud in his own voice. When he began composing the *Sonnets* he was a young man; by the time he finished composing them he was a middle-aged man. 'Young' and 'middle-aged' are relative terms but, even if it be supposed that the sonnets were composed in as short a period as ten years it will be agreed that important changes in a man's mind and personality, and so of his voice, can take place in such a period. Indeed that such a change would have to, and did, take place is the principal conclusion of the *Sonnets*. Besides, the human system, we are informed, aged more rapidly then than it does now. A middle-aged man's voice is recogniz-ably different from a young man's voice. How did the change in Shakespeare's voice alter his poetry? Or to what extent do the changes in the poetry signify changes in his voice?

In adducing examples of Shakespeare's 'I' poetry, let us re-member that to attempt to explain the *Sonnets* solely in terms of the 'Petrarchan tradition' or 'convention' is to invite failure. Such an attempt would merely lead us to ask: But what does this convention mean? Instead of being satisfied with an account of its historical origin, we would be impatient to know its psychological importance for Shakespeare. This is as much as to say that, when discussing Shakespeare's *Sonnets*, it is of little help to learn that other poets of the same period, and in several languages, wrote in a similar way. To write in a similar way is not to write in an identical way, and Shakespeare has a recog-nizable voice.

When Shakespeare was a young 'I' poet, he spoke thus:

> Those howers that with gentle worke did frame,
> The lovely gaze where every eye doth dwell
> Will play the tirants to the very same,
> And that unfaire which fairely doth excell:
> For never resting time leads Summer on,
> To hidious winter and confounds him there,
> Sap checkt with frost and lustie leav's quite gon.
> Then were not summers distillation left
> A liquid prisoner pent in walls of glasse,
> Beauties effect with beauty were bereft,
> Nor it nor noe remembrance what it was.
> > But flowers distil'd though they with winter meete,
> > Leese but their show, their substance still lives sweet.

(5)

Contrast this with the same voice eight, ten, twelve or fifteen years later:

> Those lines that I before have writ doe lie,
> Even those that said I could not love you deerer,
> Yet then my judgement knew no reason why,
> My most full flame should afterwards burne cleerer.
> But reckening time, whose million accidents
> Creepe in twixt vowes, and change decrees of Kings,
> Tan sacred beautie, blunt the sharp'st intents,
> Divert strong mindes to th' course of altring things:
> Alas why fearing of times tiranie,
> Might I not then say now I love you best,
> Crowning the present, doubting of the rest;
> > Love is a Babe, then might I not say so
> > To give full growth to that which still doth grow.

(115)

and it is apparent that the voice has altered.

Rather than spend our time in an analysis of the stylistic development that the differences between Sonnets 5 and 115 assume (for such has so often been done before, recently and notably by L. C. Knights[1]) we will rather aim at establishing the kinds of voice and vocal manner required for saying the two sonnets aloud as they ought to be said.

---

[1] In *Explorations* (Chatto & Windus, 1946), pp. 40–65.

The one and the same reader, who had successfully performed Sonnet 5, would need to make certain vocal adjustments before venturing on Sonnet 115. These adjustments would represent what had happened to Shakespeare, and to Shakespeare's voice, over a long period of time. The reader, drawing on his experience, might effect the adjustments—representing the change that in Shakespeare had taken years—in a matter of minutes or even seconds. Certainly, he would have to draw on his experience—on memory, on observation—and it is improbable that a very young reader, however adequate or admirable his rendering of 5 might be, would be able to say 115 as it ought to be said—for it would lie beyond his own experience of what time in fact does to the voice.

Now, in describing the kinds of voice required for the proper reading of 5 and 115, let us remember that such a description must necessarily undercut an analysis of stylistic features and that differences between two patterns of typography on the page exist only as signs for two contrasting patterns of sound. (That the physical change of voice expressed, or was indeed at one with, a psychological change is, of course, admitted.) Let us also remember that when we describe voices, Shakespeare's or anyone's, that we must necessarily be subjective and must hence employ metaphor. That we cannot use the language or figures of weight and mensuration is beyond regret. Metaphors are the instruments for describing the unique with any degree of precision. Weights or measures can be accurately quoted for the vocal organs extracted from cadavers, or for the sheer volume or pitch of a given sound, but are helpless in the description of a speech tone.

Shakespeare's voice in Sonnet 5—the voice we need when rendering Sonnet 5 aloud—was light. In saying 'light', as opposed to 'heavy', 'dark' or 'grave', we are already involved in metaphor. By contrast, the voice required for the reading aloud of 115, if not *basso profundo*, or even bass (and certainly it is neither of these: no Othello is talking) is yet distinctly 'darker' or deeper in pitch. The voice behind 115 is also harsher, more abrupt, stronger. The correct saying of 115 requires a sharp, a saturnine, edge to the voice which would be quite out of place in 5. Out of place and indeed impossible: for the sharp edge can only be given when the voice operates within a certain range of pitch (a middle pitch), and is 'handled' in a particular manner—the manner of Hamlet—with respect to timbre and volume.

But the voice of 5, besides being 'light', must be 'produced' softly. Imagine the lines of 5 being declaimed from a stage or a platform, and an incongruity is apparent. For, despite Sonnet 5's relation to, and similarity with, the young male lovers' speeches in *Love's Labour's Lost, Romeo and Juliet* or *Midsummer Night's Dream*, a difference is obvious. That difference points to a distinction of kind—and of practical acoustics. Sonnets, whether written by Shakespeare or by anyone else, were written not for silent reading but for performance, but for performance in conditions greatly different from those required for the performance of plays. Both were composed with the intention that they should be experienced as active sound, but whereas the sonnet was conceived as being heard from the voice of its creator—with or without a musical setting or background—by an invited company in a small chamber, the play was conceived as being heard in the large open-to-the-air public theatre.[1]

This difference in size and nature of audience and size of room meant the sonnet could be heard by those for whom it was intended to be heard even when it was sounded softly or gently, while a lover's speech in a Romantic Comedy had to be 'spoken up'. In speaking 'up', in increasing the volume of sound, beyond that needed by the audience for a sonnet, the speaker would require a slight, but decisively, different kind of 'text'. Hence, although *Love's Labour's Lost* and *Romeo and Juliet* include sonnets, a special 'quotation' manner of voice must be assumed by the players for their delivery, a 'quotation' manner distinguishable on the one hand from the manner employed for the vocal delivery of a sonnet before a select audience in a small room of the Court or a Great House (which it may parody) and, on the other hand, from the manner employed for the delivery of the surrounding dialogue, whether in rhymed or blank verse.

Not only must Sonnet 5 be spoken by a voice that either is

[1] For the whole of this question relating to the Elizabethan performance of the sonnet, see Bruce Pattison: *Music and Poetry of the English Renaissance* (Methuen, 1948).

actually, or is here for the occasion, 'light', but it must be gentle and slow. Consider the two opening lines:

> Those howers that with gentle works did frame,
> The lovely gaze where every eye doth dwell . .

and notice that the words 'gentle' and 'lovely' (adjectives which any poet nowadays would have to hurry over, or put into the implicit quotation marks of irony, or not use at all[1]) require, for their sounding, a fond, gentle, reluctant, loving lingering. Metrically ('howers' is dissyllabic), semantically and phonetically the lines ask for a soft and husky, a honeyed utterance. But so does the whole poem and so do (with merely variations within this manner) all the earlier sonnets. Meres in *Palladia Tamia* (1598) referred to them as 'sugred'. Meres meant to praise, but it is doubtful whether 'sugred' fully expresses the graceful mellifluity of the poems' movement. The voice traces, line by line, exquisite slow melodies and dwells on each cadence; it enjoys the vocalic curves it describes. Thus, if the aural pattern, or progression, of sounds described by Shakespeare's voice in 5 (or in 18 or in 33, or in almost any earlier sonnet) were recorded on, or transferred to, a musical score, no vowel would deviate, allowing its natural pitch, by more than one whole note from its predecessor or successor. Put another way: if the ten vowels (more than ten in the event of diphthongs—for a diphthong occurs when one vowel sound changes to another in the course of a single utterance) of a line in 5 were plotted, according to natural pitch, on a sheet of graph paper, then the line produced by joining up the points would show no steep peak or sharp trough. On the contrary, the melodies would trace gentle curves; and, it will be clear, that such gentle curves

---

[1] C. S. Lewis, in the chapter entitled 'Golden', in *English Literature in the Sixteenth Century* (O.U.P., 1954), pp. 319 et ff., has some admirable things to say on such adjectives as 'louely' in the poetry of Spenser's and Shakespeare's time ('Fair is as visible as green', etc.). Shakespeare could use the obvious true words like 'gentle' and 'lovely' because they were new words, i.e. they had not been used in poetry before. Donne made 'gentle' and 'lovely' impossible to use except ironically. In the eighteenth century it is possible to use 'chaste' or 'fair' again, but both in a different sense; the sense that issues from a bargain with listeners or readers to pretend in the truth of the pastoral game.

can only naturally occur when the voice proceeds at a constant and leisurely pace. The volume of the sound produced by the voice must also, in the delivery of the early sonnets, remain nearly constant: for any sudden increase or decrease of volume would alter the pitch of the sound on which the emphasis falls from its natural place in the scale and dislocate the melodic course of the entire line. For this reason there is nothing we can call dramatic about the early sonnets. Sudden variations of volume, or variations of pause lengths within the line, or of speed, or changes of mood, subject, point of view, emphasis within the line, are all dramatic—whether in the general or limited sense of the word—events. But Shakespeare in the earlier sonnets is not being 'dramatic' and his voice—whether by choice or because it had not yet mastered dramatic inflexions—avoids dramatic expedients. Hence the absence of semi-colon or full-stop within the line or almost anywhere except at the close of each quatrain when such stops coincide with the musical cadence; hence the narrow range of sentence construction; hence the prevailing pattern, on which the early sonnets are constructed, of three parallel similes; and hence the stability, in sonnet after sonnet in the early part of the series, of mood and attitude. Hence too the thematic, or continually repeated, imagery.

Elsewhere I have argued that the earlier sonnets are set in a tense which can be called the Continuous Present.[1] Shakespeare is contemplating the 'Fair Youth'. (The words 'fair' and 'youth' are not found in immediate conjunction in the *Sonnets*, I think.[2] But they occur severally and are clearly two important words throughout.) The Fair Youth is beheld from a remote yet constant distance, and his station is superior to that of the poet who beholds him, although 'station' is not intended as a metaphor for social class. Shakespeare adores, and looks up from a distance. To adore is to worship and worship

---

[1] In '"Thou" and "You" in Shakespeare's *Sonnets*' in *Poet's Grammar*, (Routledge, 1958).

[2] 'Fair youth beneath the trees. . . .' Keats brought the two words together. As a result 'youth' can now only occur in sociological reports and 'fair' in fashion notes. So far as I have been able to trace it was Israel Gollancz who first termed the object of Shakespeare's devotion 'the Fair Youth'.

leads to prayer—petitionary prayer. In course of time, the
tenor of the petitionary prayer ('hurry up and marry a girl')
alters—coinciding with an alteration of perspective and
voice—and then there is trouble. Shakespeare would like to
be the 'wife', rather than see some girl in that situation,
perhaps.

However that may be, when the writer's motive for addressing
W. H., when his ambitions or wishes, change, then Time in a
more active rôle enters. And when Time enters, bringing worry
and misery, and an anxiety to anticipate or postpone desired or
dreaded events (occasions in time), then the Continuous Present tense—altogether an ideal or Platonic tense—dissolves and
gives way to the painful tenses of actuality: past, present, future.
So it was argued.

The relevance of recalling that argument now is to point out
that when the tense, the grammatical tense, of the earlier sonnets changed, from the early Continuous Present to the tenses
denoting the actuality of time, then that change was accompanied by a changed physical voice. Pitch, timbre, the inflexions or tones of a mature voice, cannot be explained without
reference to the history of the speaker. Unless a speaker has a
history—has acquired, that is, some experience—he cannot
inflect the grammatical forms denoting the tense of a verb with
appropriate tones. The speaker cannot expressively speak
about time until he has suffered from time, and the linguistic
instrument for expressing the effects of time is grammatical
tense. In the middle or later sonnets, where Shakespeare talks
as one who knows about the effects of time, the monotoned
voice of the early sonnets gives way to a voice owning mastery
of a variety of tones; and a glance at 115, quoted above, will
reveal that what controls the tones are the changes in Verb
Forms, such forms themselves signalizing the irresistible operations of time.

It might be retorted that the irresistible operations of time
are stated, or threatened, in even the earliest sonnets such as
our 5. It is mainly in the sestets of the early sonnets that the
statement or threat occurs. But the statement or threat in the
sestets of the early sonnets is not *felt*. It is in the sestets that the
predicates are made. Nevertheless the lovely subject of these
predicates remains unscathed in the octave of the sonnet because

those predicates are, in truth, but theoretical at this stage. As here:

> Loe in the Orient when the gracious light,
> Lifts up his burning head, each under eye
> Doth homage to his new appearing sight,
> Serving with lookes his sacred majesty,
> And having climb'd the steepe up heavenly hill,
> Resembling strong youth in his middle age,
> Yet mortall lookes adore his beauty still,
> Attending on his goulden pilgrimage:
> But when from high-most pich with wery car,
> Like feeble age he reeleth from the day,
> The eyes (fore dutious) now converted are
> From his low tract and looke on other way:
> So thou, thy selfe out-going in thy noon:
> Unlok'd on diest unlesse thou get a sonne.

(7)

We have said that the level of the voice in the earlier sonnets is constant. This is so, provided that by 'constant' it is realized we do not mean that Shakespeare speaks in a flat level voice. In fact, that one can refer to the melodies, the undulations (however gentle), shows that 'constant' is not meant to imply a plane of speech pitch, but rather that the pitch curves are gentle curves, and that the range of pitch in any one of the early sonnets is narrow. By contrast, the later sonnets show the most abrupt, or dramatic, peaks and troughs in the line of pitch. We suggest that the sudden, and so dramatic, fluctuations of pitch and tone, necessitated indeed by changes in tenses, in the later sonnets were prepared for, or anticipated, in the *sestets* of the earlier sonnets—not in the octaves.

Reference to Sonnets 5 or to 12, 18, 77, will show chance, but conspicuous examples, of a general tendency: that Shakespeare's voice after the completion of the octave (sometimes as early as after the opening six lines) tends to drop to a graver note.

Not that the octave of these, and of other earlier sonnets, is—in contrast with the sestet—devoid of melancholy. In every line of each unit of the entire sequence there is melancholy. Melancholy threads and absorbs and wraps the *Sonnets*, but we would do wrong to suppose that all kinds of melancholy speak in grave

129

notes, notes low in the vocal scale. There is melancholy and melancholy, and the melancholy of the octaves of the earliest sonnets is as sweet as it is bitter. But why is it sweet at all?—and why, being so, must it be planed high in the vocal scale? The answer, possibly, is this: Despite the vast space separating the poet from his 'ideal'; despite the elevation separating the adored from the adorer; despite these obstacles (let alone the sameness of sex)—obstacles which perhaps ought to have prevented small desires growing into greater at the outset—Shakespeare, in the octaves, and within the tensal frame of a Continuous Present, insistently and obstinately ventures a kind of hope. Within the frame of that tense (the tense of hope is the Future), he prospects (for only that tense is amenable to this sort of play); there he prospects or postulates possibilities of possession or enjoyment. But in the sestet, as a rule, the hope is cautioned, or is shown to be false, as the timelessness of the Continuous Present is confronted with actual (or real) time expressed by tenses in the Indicative—Present, Future, Past. As that happens the pitch of Shakespeare's voice drops or deepens, confessing those checks to hope.

It is in the sestets of the earlier sonnets that the rose, so admired in the octave, is admitted to have a term to its life. In the sestet the rose—however fair it is, or *was* a minute ago in the octave—*will* droop, wither and die. In the sestet the glorious morning of love *will* become overcast; in the sestet the fair early summer of the octave *will* decline into winter; it is in the sestet that the beauty of the youth, celebrated in the octave, *will* become ravaged by time and *will* become sunk in 'age's sleepy night'. The earlier Shakespeare sonnet is thus constructed on a dialectic based on grammatical tense. The octave tense is in a kind of Present, the sestet envisages a future when this Present will be reckoned as a Past. But this must not be taken too narrowly: it is simply the norm. Sometimes the Future tense, saying that all this beauty now so perfect *will* be rendered imperfect by time, begins its warning and its realization not in the ninth but the sixth or the thirteenth line; at other times the Present tense pays its homage to the *now*, and the Future its warning of the *to be*, within a single quatrain of the octave. But these are departures from a norm in which the formal divisions, octave and sestet, express two kinds of time.

Even this, it might be objected, is too summary, and some would argue that the average early sonnet is in three parts: (i) an act of homage to present beauty, (ii) a realization of its decay in the future, and (iii) an act of consolation—as, for example, when the young man is told he will be immortalized in poetry.

There is force in this objection, but it should be remembered that this third part, the consolation—enjoying its own kind of tense, and at first said in a voice confident, even vaunting— becomes increasingly perfunctory as the sequence progresses. Shakespeare becomes less convinced of the worth or reality of such consolations, and the third part can shrivel to the dimensions of a concluding couplet, e.g.

> Yet doe thy worst ould Time dispight thy wrong,
> My love shall in my verse ever live young.
>
> (19)

and later disappear altogether. Hence the general truth of the rule: in the earlier sonnets the octave is a statement of beauty existing and adored now, the sestet is a counter-statement of the certain destruction of that beauty in the future.

Now although the grave intent of the sestet would be fore-known even at the outset of the octave (thus tingeing even the adoration of present beauty with melancholy and so creating this sense and sound of bitter sweetness or sweet bitterness), yet the change from octave to sestet corresponds with a change in Shakespeare's voice to which a modern listener and reciter must react. Narrow though the vocal scale of the earlier sonnets may be, Shakespeare's voice yet tends to move to a graver or darker note in the ninth line. Why the different grammatical tenses, expressing different spiritual conditions of the speaker, should require correspondingly different vocal tones and pitch is a problem it is hoped to resume later. Meanwhile, it is our suggestion that it was through his realization of the menace of actual time, as he expressed it in the sestets of the earlier, but in the whole body of the later, sonnets, that Shakespeare extended the range of his personal voice and increasingly exercised it in the expression of new tones. These tones were generally inimical to the lighter earlier Romantic Comedies (set like the octaves of the early sonnets either outside or in their own time[1]) but are appropriate for the delivery of much of the dialogue in the time-ridden history plays. This amounts to saying that the force and intention of the sound and meaning of the early sestets worked upon and gradually subsumed the lighter golden notes of the early octaves and so led to the deeper voice of Shakespeare's mature period.

That deeper voice is speaking behind 115 (quoted on p. 123 above). Though deeper it is by no means extraordinarily weighty, full or rounded. Nor is it any longer light or golden. The spiritual state, the disposition of mind, the Continuous Present tense, all demanding a light golden voice, have gone. One is left in the situation of wondering which went first: whether the alteration in personality (as a consequence of the dethronement of hope and the entry into a new phase of being) occasioned or followed a change in the physical voice.

Some might think this: Since Shakespeare's voice was essentially the creative agent of an 'I' poet, then, as that voice naturally deepened with age, so its owner naturally shifted the tone and character of his poetry to harmonize with it. Whatever the case, all would recognize the profound mutual influence exerted upon each other by mind and body, and all would admit the voice to be the issue of both. Additionally, all would recognize a kind of parallelism or dialogue between the series of sonnets and the plays completed by 1600 or 1603.

iii

Shakespeare was, and is, unique among the great English poets (the Elizabethan dramatists not excluded) in that he created the great bulk of his work not in terms of his own voice, nor for himself to speak, but for the voices of a group or team of men and boys whose voices he came to know so well as to prefer

---

[1] Although one comedy at least, *Love's Labour's Lost*, moves like a sonnet and actual time comes to invade Act V. The Messenger brings news of the death of the Princess's father. Thereon 'the Scene begins to cloud' (cp. Sonnet 33) and at the end of the play we are told:

> The words of Mercurie
> Are harsh after the songs of Apollo.

to exploit them before his own.[1] This is a primary fact, but the force of a primary fact is (*because* primary it is taken for granted) frequently more difficult to realize than the existence of subordinate facts. But admittance of this primary fact opens a discussion as to whether it was for one voice, or three, or eight, or sixteen (outside his own) for which Shakespeare *chiefly* created, which he chiefly sensed, imagined and exploited.

The list of the names of the 'Principall Actors' prefixed to the First Folio; that cast printed before the text of *Everyman in his Humour*; those biographical fragments relating to all the known professional players of the period given in the second volume of E. K. Chambers' *The Elizabethan Stage*; those scraps of information revealed in Commendatory Verses; those traditionary tales —are all insufficient for determining the exact number and identities of the precise instruments (voices) for whom Shakespeare conceived at any one period. Which parts he designed for which actors, among that list of 'Principall Actors', as he wrote play after play between 1590 and 1611, and the extent to which his design was gratified in performances during his working career, are questions to which many would like to know the answers. But certain and complete answers, based on documentary evidence, will never be yielded, though partial answers might.

Meanwhile we can be thankful for the meagre documentary knowledge we possess. We *know* that Kempe played Peter in *Romeo and Juliet* and Dogberry in *Much Ado*;[2] we know that Slye played Verges; and some of us will think that the evidence that Richard Burbage played Richard III, 'young Hamlett', 'kind Leir' and 'the greued Moore' is sufficient.[3]

Then there are the traditions which we may accept or reject. The tradition that Shakespeare played Old Adam in *As You Like It* and the Ghost in *Hamlet*; the tradition that Armin played Falstaff, the rival tradition that Burbage did.

The rest is speculation. We might like to attach 'old stuttering' Heminges to the parts of Leonato in *Much Ado* or The

---

[1] Shakespeare was unique in this for reasons set out on p. 118 above. Other Elizabethan and Jacobean dramatists (except Nathan Field) were not permanent members of a company; they were freelances.

[2] E. K. Chambers, *op. cit.*, II, p. 326.

[3] *Ibid.*, II, pp. 308–309, for a discussion of the evidence.

Exiled Duke in *As You Like It,* and to trace his previous parts back to Old Capulet from these rôles; and we might—in our minds—discern 'a lineage' of rôles (from one play to another between 1594 and 1611) for other of the 'Principall Actors' of the Chamberlain's Men. We might, for example, feel convinced that Augustine Phillips played part *a* in play x and part *b* in play y, and perceive a relation between these parts suggesting that they were designed for the same player, but such a conjecture would have no support external to our interpretations of parts *a* and *b* (however close the resemblance between the parts might then appear) and a respect for probabilities.

Shakespeare's fellows—the solid core of adult actors, his vocal resources, his instruments, from year in and year out between 1594 and 1611—were important. For had their personalities been other than they were, then Shakespeare's work would have been other than it is. Yet only in one respect were they perhaps more important than the prentices, the boys with their 'soft pipes', for whom the parts of Hero, Rosalind and Viola were conceived, in the respect that they were permanent members, whereas the prentices, as boy players undertaking female rôles, had an acting career of only a few years—the years of adolescence during which, in voice and physique, they changed rapidly. But Shakespeare's feeling, between 1598 and 1600, for the boys pretending to be girls dressed up as boys (Ganymede, Cesario) was different from his feeling, between 1606 and 1611, for the boys who played the part of adored and all-treasured daughters (Cordelia, Marina, Perdita, Miranda). A succession of prentices might perhaps have been more important to Shakespeare—first, possibly as figures for W. H. and later, possibly, as figures for the poet's younger daughter—in his private emotional life than was Burbage. Against this, in the practical life, Burbage became Shakespeare's chief surrogate, possessing capacities of voice far superior to Shakespeare's.

iv

Shakespeare did not 'learn' to employ or command voices other than his own quickly or easily. In the case of the earliest comedies it is hardly an exaggeration to say that he wrote the whole of them in terms of one voice, his own, and then distributed it among the characters. Certainly, the melody of no line is exactly repeated, but the melodies of a great number of lines are all very much alike. And the melodies of the lines of the early comedies are much like the exquisite melodies of the earlier sonnets. The melodies of the earlier sonnets and the earlier plays belong to a *genre*. Shakespeare at this time—because aware of, and mastering, his own voice—tends to restrict his *dramatis personae* to a single age group—his own. We cite *Love's Labour's Lost* as an example. There the men and women who speak their lines of 'honey'd eloquence' are enjoying, or playing, the same Act of Life (the third of the seven, that of the Lover in Jacques' well-known speech) as the writer of the early sonnets. Outside this group, the Braggart, and the other type figures of Plautian Comedy may seem either older or simply ageless in their voices as they conduct a dialogue and action that is partially destructive of the dream of Romantic Love in which the Courtiers are involved. It is from the friction, generated by this conflict between the golden voice of the lover (here Shakespeare's, of the early sonnets, distributed among others of either sex) and the ageless voices of experienced folly, that Shakespeare's development is to proceed.[1] That development is to amount to a control by Shakespeare of voices other than his own as well as an enlargement of his own. Meanwhile, the speeches of the lovers, or of their friends of the same age, in the earlier comedies, can almost be interchanged among themselves with hardly any violence to character, and sometimes scarcely even to plot, and none to voice. Not merely could Navarre and Berowne, or Romeo and Benvolio exchange, but Berowne and Rosaline, or Romeo and Juliet, could frequently exchange speeches since their voices are not imagined as essentially differentiated.

In Act IV of *Love's Labour's Lost* we hear the lovers' sonnets. Of these, Longueville's

> Did not the heavenly Rhetoricke of thine eye . . .[2]

and Berowne's

> If love makes me forsworn, how shall I swere to love?[3]

---

[1] The voice of the 'low' comic character seeks to have a corrosive effect on the illusions of the lover that is analogous to the effect of the sestet in the *Sonnets* on the premises of the octave.

[2] Act IV, sc. iii, 60.   [3] IV, ii, 109.

appear in the *Passionate Pilgrime*, 1599, but they could equally
well have appeared in the *Sonnets* of 1609. So might the King's
sonnet

> So sweet a kiss the golden sun gives not . . . .[1]

Now how are such sonnets to be distinguished by their vocal
delivery from their context of ordinary dialogue? or not quite
ordinary dialogue since in *Love's Labour's Lost*—and in *Romeo and
Juliet* likewise—Shakespeare generally seems intent on applying
lyrical patterns to dramatic verse? How does Berowne, by its
delivery, distinguish his sonnet from such a speech as

> My eyes are then no eyes, nor I *Berowne*.
> O, but for my Love day would turne to night,
> Of all complexions the cul'd sovereignty
> Doe meet as at a faire in her faire cheeke,
> Where severall Worthies make one dignity,
> Where nothing wants, that want it selfe doth seeke . . .[2]

which it so much resembles in pitch, tone and melody?

The answer would be that, when the King and his three com-
panions start *reading* their sonnets, they deliberately adopt a
'reading' or 'quotation' tone. How is such a tone produced in
actual practice? By a pause before the quoted material? By an
accentuation of the sonnet's rhyme pattern and of its other
formal features? By an alteration in pitch and speed?[3]

To such an account of how the King and his three courtiers
produce the change from the dramatic (or stage-delivery)
manner to the sonnet-reading manner we should add that the
King and his courtiers do not *read* their sonnets aloud from the
stage in exactly the same manner as we can suppose Shakespeare *performed* his own sonnets. For one thing, Navarre and his
friends are supposed not so much to be performing as to be overheard by the audience, and by each other, while they 'read

---

[1] Act IV, iii, 26.   [2] IV, iii, 232–237.

[3] This reading tone of the King and his courtiers in *Love's Labour's Lost*
is to be distinguished from the 'inset' tone of, say, the Fool in *Lear* when he
reels off gnomic verses. The Fool reels off lines to whose proverbial substance the audience had long given its assent. The mnemonic train, like the
well-worn gramophone record, is started and off the lines go. Performance
over, the Fool returns to his individual voice.

through'—or test—their compositions; for another, the acoustics of the public theatre, or of the hall of a Great House (if we feel compelled to accept the conclusions of Miss Yates that it was for private performance that *Love's Labour's Lost* was designed[1]), must be regarded as distinct from the acoustics of the sort of chamber most favourably constructed for the reception of a sonnet; for another—subject again to Miss Yates' conclusions—the size and composition of the audience for this play would be larger and more diverse in class and interests than the audience for a sonnet.

Nevertheless, with all this in mind, we are still almost obliged, I think, to agree that the distributed personal voice of Shakespeare is almost the only voice offered and heard in the verse of *Two Gentlemen of Verona, Romeo and Juliet, Love's Labour's Lost* and *Midsummer Night's Dream*—the exception being the voices of the low or comic characters of the clowns. Not in verse but in the *prose* of the Mechanicals in *A Midsummer Night's Dream*, Shakespeare, more decisively than in *Love's Labour's Lost*, clearly or positively begins to catch the accents, to imagine, apprehend and echo, voices—real voices—outside his own for the first time. And if it was in and through prose—not verse—that Shakespeare heard and makes us hear the voices of others, then it was through prose (and not verse) that he attained that capaciousness of being whereby he was enabled to enter—and absorb so as to speak for, or rather bespeak—the beings of others.

Thus, whereas the voices of the four romantic lovers in *A Midsummer Night's Dream* can hardly be differentiated from each other, or from the personal voice of the early sonnets, the Mechanicals, on the contrary, own voices that Shakespeare had not controlled before. Nor is it simply a collective 'other voice' that they own and use, for Bottom's voice is distinguished from that of Quince and the voice of Flute—since Flute is chosen to play Thisbe, and since all actors are agreed as to how both Flute and Flute playing Thisbe are to be spoken—is distinguished from either. Here is a test that Shakespeare's mute signs nevertheless convey three distinct voices: in every revival of the play the player of Quince assumes the quavering accents of an old man, Bottom the full-bodied voice of a man in middle life,

[1] See F. A. Yates, *A Study of Love's Labour's Lost* (C.U.P. 1936).

Flute a voice which can strike a falsetto it can hardly maintain. But the differences between these three voices have not *only* to be accepted on a basis that certain voices are appropriate to certain personalities and actions. For here the phonetics, the arrangement of the signs for sounds accords with what may be inferred from plot and character.

Yet though it was through prose, as being nearer to the daily speech he was likely to hear, that Shakespeare first conveyed vocal identity outside himself, he became in time able to apply this power to characters who spoke in verse, beginning perhaps with Shylock. We say 'apply'. More exactly, it was a transference of a skill at listening, proper to the artist of fictional or dramatic prose, to an essentially different, even opposite, medium—opposite because it usually calls on the poet to regard his personal voice as instrument. Except in the dedications to *Venus* and *Lucrece*, all the early prose of Shakespeare is the prose not of one speaking in his own person but a listener's prose, of one who listens and then 'takes off' or burlesques what he has heard.

How and when did this event begin? Whatever is suggested in way of answer, we should remember that in 1594 Lord Strange's was reconstituted as the Lord Chamberlain's Men, and that it was only after this date that Shakespeare was free to compose plays with reference to a thoroughly settled company and a knowledge that particular parts would be played by particular men. In composing *A Midsummer Night's Dream* he was able to conceive of Bottom being spoken by—let us suppose—Kempe and to be fairly assured in advance that Bottom would really be played by Kempe.[1] From this vantage he would be able to count on Kempe's peculiar vocal resources and so exploit them—instead of imagining a voice in the slight hope that some player or other would be able to realize it aloud. Nevertheless Shakespeare, in imaginatively entering the being of Kempe so as to employ the vocal resources of Kempe (if it was Kempe), modified Kempe—for an actor, it is reasonable to suppose, is permanently influenced to some extent by the parts he has played. But Kempe also modified Shakespeare, for

[1] Supposition: but an instance was needed, and in tracing lineages it is not unreasonable to suppose that the player of Dogberry had played Bottom four years previously.

Shakespeare created Bottom in terms of—and through—
Kempe and no one is unaffected by his own achievements.

Whether there were any specific models for Bottom or Quince
or Flute among the artisans of Warwickshire or London, we
cannot possibly say. Probably not. What goes to make them was
more likely selected—after a process of listening, observation,
imagination, empathy—from Shakespeare's whole experience
of an order of human beings, the artisan class. Or perhaps it
was a case where the experience of a class of men suddenly
seemed to personalize and represent itself in a particular
example. But whether there were living prototypes for these
'low comic' characters outside the theatre or not, the fact is
that those characters could not have made themselves heard
in the theatre except instrumentally through actors like
Kempe.

But why did Shakespeare catch the voice of Kempe or the
voices of artisans sufficiently for later players to be able to reproduce them from the printed signs? Conceiving the parts of
Proteus, Berowne, Romeo or Lysander, he was largely confined by his experience as the 'I' of the earlier sonnets. Against
this limitation, though unable himself to speak in the voices of
robust middle-aged, or frail elderly, artisans (though Kempe
could), he could yet listen to what they said. And what they
said they said in prose, and their prose conveys nearly the whole
of life outside the romantic, the platonic, the idealistic: rather,
it conveys the opposites of these, the down-to-earth, the appeti-
tive, the instinctual. The timbre of the voices which said such
prose was harsh and strong, far removed from the timbre of the
voice of the sonnets or Romeo. That timbre conditioned the
language. The 'diction of common life',[1] of which the earlier
sonnets and the romantic lovers seem ignorant, is naturally
spoken by the early comic characters. Though it might be
thought that only such characters (possessing such voices)
could employ such diction, yet, somewhere between 1598 and
1600, Shakespeare's tragic poetry began to absorb elements of
precisely that language which previously had been confined to
his speakers of comic prose. In absorbing these elements, and
absorbing them with increasing ease and mastery, Shakespeare's

[1] See F. P. Wilson, *Shakespeare and the Diction of Common Life* (Proceedings
of the British Academy, XXVII, 1941).

poetry not only gained in range and power but it gained voices. Shakespeare's personal voice no doubt, on the evidence of the later sonnets (which no less than the dramatic poetry had absorbed elements of the diction of common life), had itself increased in range and flexibility. But though Shakespeare, when the time came, might have been able to have voiced the part of Hamlet it is doubtful whether he could have been the physical organ for Claudius and Polonius as well, let alone Lear. The kind and variety of voices, assumed by the mature and later plays, suggests that Shakespeare's poetry had grown beyond Shakespeare's own vocal resources and that he became dependent on men like Burbage as instruments and surrogates. But the *origin* of that astonishing growth may well have been the prose-speaking voices of artisans which were heard and echoed for the benefit of the actors of early comic parts.

v

Earlier we suggested that the romantic lovers of the early plays, all the young men even (the rôle of the young man is to be, if not a lover, then the lover's friend and abettor)—Valentine, Berowne, Longueville and Dumaine; Romeo and Benvolio; Lysander and Demetrius, etc.—spoke with one voice and in one kind of voice—physical voice—and that this voice was essentially Shakespeare's own in the earlier sonnets. In attempting to define that voice we said it was high in pitch and soft in timbre. Employing metaphors, it was a light, golden voice; the voice not only of the wooer but of the courtier. These romantic lovers did not flatly say their words nor yet indeed quite sing them, but breathed them out with a soft yet pulsating ardour. They sounded forth exquisite melodies into the air and seemed conscious enough of them to wish to linger over them. Their conscious delight in the melodies they traced, and their tremulous ardour, compelled a leisurely delivery— leisurely in contrast with, say, Hamlet when, like a whore, he unpacks his heart with words, or with Iago when, at the outset of the play, he rattles out to Roderigo the reasons for his hatred of Othello. Let us give instances of the voice of the young lover.

Here's Proteus:

> Oh, how this Spring of love resembleth
> The uncertain glory of an Aprill day,
> Which now shewes all the beauty of the Sun,
> And by and by a cloud takes all away.[1]

and here Berowne:

> For Valour, is not Love a *Hercules*?
> Still climbing trees in the *Hesperides*.
> Subtill as Sphinx, as sweet and musicall,
> As bright *Apollo's* Lute, strung with his haire.
> And when Love speakes, the voyce of all the Gods,
> Make heaven drowsie with the harmonie.[2]

Bassanio:

> In Belmont is a Lady richly left,
> And she is faire, and fairer then that word,
> Of wondrous vertues, sometimes from her eyes
> I did receive faire speechlesse messages . . .[3]

Here's Romeo (with Rosaline in mind):

> These happy maskes that kisse faire Ladies browes,
> Being blacke, puts us in mind they hide the faire:
> He that is strooken blind, cannot forget
> The precious treasure of his eye-sight lost:
> Shew me a Mistresse that is passing faire
> What doth her beauty serve but as a note,
> Where I may read who past that passing faire.[4]

And Romeo (on Juliet):

> O she doth teach the Torches to burne bright:
> It seemes she hangs upon the cheeke of night,
> As a rich Jewel in an Æthiops eare:
> Beauty too rich for use, for earth too deare:
> So shewes a Snowy Dove trooping with Crowes,
> As yonder Lady ore her fellowes showes;

[1] *Two Gentlemen of Verona*, I, iii, 84–87.
[2] *Love's Labour's Lost*, IV, iii, 340–345.
[3] *Merchant of Venice*, I, i, 161–164.
[4] *Romeo and Juliet*, I, i, 236–242.

> The measure done, Ile watch her place of stand,
> And touching hers, make blessed my rude hand.
> Did my heart love till now, forsweare it sight,
> For I never saw true Beauty till this night.[1]

And here's Shakespeare (in his best-known sonnet):

> Shall I compare thee to a Summers day?
> Thou art more lovely and more temperate . . .[2]

Granting that the four dramatic characters speak in much the same voice and that this voice is essentially that of the young amorous Shakespeare's (but allowing simply for the difference of acoustics between public theatre and a chamber suitable for the recital of sonnets), we ask why this should be?

The question is important when we remember that a complete answer would go far to explain why the whole of Shakespeare's earlier work—with the vital exception of the Histories —should be as it actually is—a vision, or study, of Romantic Love. For each play of this period (except the Histories) takes its dominant vocal tone or colouring from its hero who speaks in a kind of voice suitable to his amorous mission. But why does a special kind of mission require a special kind of voice for its literal *ex*pression?

The question is addressed not only to Shakespeare's psychology—and physiology, since the voice in action is eminently the expression of both soul and body being jointly employed—but to our own. That it is also our own can be verified by enquiries of any theatrical producer—whether professional or amateur— of any of the early Romantic Comedies or of the one Romantic Tragedy.

To confine ourselves to the Romantic Tragedy. Each of these theatrical producers would say that the player of Romeo must be a *light tenor* whose voice can naturally intone those lines where the phonetics, the *vocables*, those high notes of the middle register, express the condition of aspiring love.

Not that Romeo throughout the whole of the play maintains the high, soft, ardent notes of his early scenes. He drops his voice by as much perhaps as two whole notes when he exclaims on the miseries of banishment in Act III, sc. iii; and, when he hears of Juliet's death in Act V, sc. i, the whole cast and timbre

---

[1] *Romeo and Juliet*, I, v, 46–55.   [2] Sonnet 18.

of it changes. It becomes harsh in command. When he remembers the Apothecary's shop:

> I do remember An Appothecarie,
> And here abouts 'a dwells, which late I noted
> In tattred weeds, with overwhelming browes,
> Culling of Simples, meager were his lookes . . .
>
> (V, i, 37–40)

or when he rewards him:

> There's thy Gold,
> Worse poyson to mens soules,
> Doing more murther in this loathsome world,
> Then these poore compounds that thou maiest not sell.
> I sell thee poyson, thou hast sold me none . . .
>
> (V, i, 79–83)

or when he adumbrates his own end, it gains new, awful and
leaden tones. In such tragic scenes it becomes resonant, sometimes sepulchral, sometimes richer, but always deeper and fuller
than would have ever seemed possible from the earlier scenes
when he was apostrophizing Rosaline or Juliet.

But this deep plunge of Romeo's voice—anticipating the
normal pitch of the heroes of the great Tragedies—in its despair and suicidal resolution, distinguishes it and its owner
from the earlier Romeo when he was aspiring for possession of
his beloved like the Romantic Lover of the Comedies, and this
distinction suggests an explanation as to why the Romantic
Lover—until, and unless, he actually finds himself in the position of Romeo in Act V—ought to have a light, soft voice.
Ought? *Must* rather, because the properties of the speeches
Shakespeare wrote for him (and sounded within himself) demand such a voice; *must*, because Shakespeare's conception of
the voice proper to the Romantic Lover has the support of
general human psychology. The stage tradition (in all operas
that readily come to mind the *inamorato* is a tenor and the
middle-aged villain a bass-baritone) is founded on common
psychology as exemplified by Shakespeare.

It is the natural disposition of the young man to be in love. If
he is not actually in love, the young man yet has the will to be
so—as Romeo, say, had the *will* to be in love with Rosaline (or

with any one) before he actually fell in love with Juliet. Now the early Romantic Comedies of Shakespeare and the first half of *Romeo and Juliet* are concerned—this, indeed, is their concern —to reveal young men in love.

But to be in love is to be in a state not of possession but of desire, and so restlessness. In the Comedies when the object of desire is attained (in *Love's Labour's Lost* the attainment is postponed; merely postponed, for to suppose final loss in place of postponement is to be overharsh), or when the attainment is promised, or assured, the play comes to an end. Now though a state of desire is a state of unrest, and though the person in a state of desire is not content with his present position in time but looks towards the future for the satisfaction of his hopes, we need not overstress his torment. We need not stress it, if only because the Romantic Comedy promises that the torment will end with possession and all unrest will cease with satisfaction of hopes—*all* unrest, for it is a further premise of this *genre* that possession of the mistress brings heaven. And what is heaven but a complete satisfaction, with no further motive for unrest (no further desire), an absolute of joy.[1] The tradition of Romantic Comedy supposes a termination of the torment of longing, and of all other torment, with the possession of a desired person. Shakespeare's Human Comedy, like Dante's Divine Comedy, premises an end of desire in perfect fulfilment. But there is this difference: experience, and the philosopher, would discountenance the former as an illusion.

Yet it is no illusion to Proteus, Valentine; to Berowne, Dumaine, Longueville; to Lysander, Demetrius; to Bassanio. The plays in which they occur show young men aspiring[2] towards attainable objects—Sylvia, Portia and the rest. These young men are, one and all, in the spiritual condition of hope. What they hope for is, because of the terms of a dramatic convention, possible to themselves and to us—the audience; more than

---

[1] In the lines from *East Coker*

The torment
Of love unsatisfied, the greater torment
Of love satisfied

the 'torment' has a degree of seriousness with which we are not here concerned.

[2] From *ad-spirare*, literally a breathing themselves *to*wards a good.

possible, certain. They will certainly finally possess those to whom they aspire though—equally certainly—only after trials and delays.

But the state of hope—like the state of its opposite, despair—has its real and revealing voice. Shakespeare speaks, and we speak, of the 'leaden accents of despair' (we hear them, indeed, from Hamlet), but hope no less reveals itself in 'accents', i.e. in pitch, timbre, intonation. A man in a state of desire, who also believes he will get what he desires, speaks in thrilling and eager tones. The tones are eager because the speaker, not content with—or in—his present, but hopefully confident of his future, is projecting himself in the future, and 'transported beyond the ignorant present' he feels 'the future in an instant'. His voice is high in pitch because he is exalted and aspiring. The literal meanings of *exalted* and *aspiring*, descriptive of emotional mood or spiritual state, are in fact geared to the vocal scale and, as metaphors, are perhaps derived from it. The Romantic Lover, i.e. the man not in possession, but in pursuit or expectation, of a real or supposed good, looks towards the future and his voice rises to meet it. He lives in a state of hope. By contrast, the *dejected* or *depressed* man (again we should realize literal meanings: such a man is thrust down and is feeling 'low'), the man in a state of despair, registers his state of being through his voice. He speaks in flat and leaden accents. Timbre and pitch reveal his condition.

But whereas the romantic lovers in the early comedies (and perhaps Shakespeare too in the earliest sonnets) expected success and (though not Shakespeare) won it, albeit in *Love's Labour's Lost* after a year's delay, Romeo has a different career. He gained the object of his aspiration,[1] not in Act V as do the lovers in the Comedies, but betimes in Act III. Romeo consummates his love, and then experiences first banishment and then despair. Romeo's voice traces the contours of his career—aspiration, brief joy of possession, dejection in consequence of an enforced parting. Romeo suffers a reversal of fortune, and in vocally expressing that reversal Shakespeare was to venture on an exploration of the dynamics of the lower half of the vocal

---

[1] The pictorial effect of the balcony scene (Act II, sc. ii) is an exact equivalent for its vocal accompaniment. Romeo aspires towards Juliet and there she is visibly poised above him.

scale such as he was to undertake more thoroughly later in the Great Tragedies.[1] In such lines of Romeo's as:

> I do remember An Appothecarie,
> And here abouts 'a dwells . . .[2]

or:

> Death that hath suckt the honey of thy breath,
> Hath had no power yet upon thy Beautie:
> Thou are not conquer'd: Beauties ensigne yet
> Is Crymson in thy lips, and in thy cheekes,
> And Deaths pale flag is not advanced there.[3]

we can say that Shakespeare, though writing appropriately for a company that in 1594 was almost wholly as young as himself, was beginning to foreshadow a dramatic progress which was to correspond with his own and his actors' vocal growth—*beginning* to foreshadow, for the *vocables* of Romeo's lines just quoted still reveal a voice that is young, however sunk or dejected.

The early comedies (and the first three acts of *Romeo*) have in fact plots with a romantic love motive requiring one vocal pitch above all others. When Shakespeare came to *Antony and Cleopatra* it was a different matter. But we cannot conclude this section without reference to the Histories. For the young military hero no less than the romantic lover is forward-looking. He looks towards 'Honour', instead of towards a mistress, as an entity to be pursued and possessed. No less is his spiritual condition one of hope,[4] and like the lover the vocal pitch in which he declares his aims is high in the scale. There is this difference: it is not only high but, unlike the lover's, it has a hard edge. The timbre of the soldier is different from the wooer's. Henry V speaks like a clarion.

To an objection that we have been labouring to say what common sense already allows—namely, that a wooer speaks wooingly and that a sad man speaks sadly (and it is that which guides a theatrical producer when he is casting a play)—we

---

[1] I am aware that in *Richard II* Shakespeare's main figure has a voice which traverses a wide range, moving from high-pitched petulance to deep melancholy.

[2] Act V, sc. i, 37, 38.   [3] Act V, sc. iii, 92–96.

[4] The general relevance of this to the essay on Shelley above will be clear.

would reply that our enquiry has shown that particular emotional states of being require not only an appropriate colouring of tone but also an appropriate pitch or norm of pitch.

That in itself is a discovery. But it does not stop there. The norm of pitch, judged as appropriate to an emotional state of being, must be selected with a reference to the age of the speaker. Romeo and Antony are alike at some points of their careers in being unsatisfied lovers. But Romeo (in, say, the balcony scene Act II, sc. i) voices his unsatisfied longing in a golden and ardent pitch of the top register. Antony—because of his age, because of his physical bulk, because of his experience (which means that he has memories of earlier 'affairs', and a knowledge of the limits of peace to be derived from 'affairs' however attractive and interesting the present 'affair' in comparison with others hitherto may be), because of all of these working in combination—voices his longing in a norm of pitch that may be high for him—but too low for the top register. (The same difference of register applies *mutatios mutandis* to Henry V and Coriolanus.)

Troilus, in his voice as in other respects, comes between Romeo and Antony. Let us realize here that Troilus was not the coeval of Shakespeare as Romeo and Antony were Shakespeare's coevals when he respectively created these. Young Troilus' romantic longing had to be vocally created through memory, and, though the infidelity he suffered might have been analogous to something the dramatist had recently endured, he had to give *this* too a shrillness from the powers of memory.

Further, we see that when a wooer speaks wooingly, or when a sad man speaks sadly, it is because wooer and sad man not only express their states by tone and pitch but also by tropes, imagery and particular grammatical inflexions and syntactical constructions appropriate to these contrasting emotional states and which render their vocalization the easier.

vi

It would seem, then, that there is a correlation between natural vocal pitch and either a person's age or his state of being—or to both, since a person's state of being is frequently conditioned by his age.

Thus, a young man tends to be in love, or to fall in love, and to be in love is to be in a certain state of being, a state of hope which is a looking towards the future. So much we have deduced from a consideration of the voice or voices of the romantic lovers in Shakespeare's early plays. Their speeches (with the exception of Romeo's in his suicidal despair[1]) have to be delivered in a high, soft, vibrant voice if they are to be delivered at all in accordance either with the linguistic sounds proclaimed by the text or with their spirit. The sounds and the spirit agree with theatrical tradition and our knowledge of psychology alike. But since the whole intention of these early romantic plays (again *Romeo and Juliet* is an exception) is one of satisfaction of hope, a fulfilment of romantic desire (the whole strategy of plot administering to that and centring on the fortunes of the lovers), it must be admitted that this is the primary intention of Shakespeare at this period. Or, to translate 'intention' into 'action': The action of Shakespeare, in his early period, is the action of romantic desire and this desire requires a special level of the voice. His early romantic heroes speak at that level. I suggest, on the evidence of the early sonnets, that it was the level of Shakespeare's own voice at this period, and that he lent it, or distributed it, among his romantic heroes.

We now come to Shakespeare's voice, and the voice of his surrogates, in his middle or mature period.

First, it must be remembered, that while Shakespeare, in the comedies, had distributed his own voice (as he heard it) among the romantic lovers and courtiers, there began to emerge in those plays certain autonymous voices. Such voices, echoed or enacted by 'low' or comic members of the Chamberlain's Men, presumably had, as their originals, the voices of countrymen or artisans. The comedians of the Chamberlain's Men became vehicles for a selected and typified (for only gradually does the comic character become more of an individual than a representative) speech which Shakespeare remembered hearing in the country or listened to in London. These 'heard' or external voices are distinguishable from Shakespeare's personal voice—distinguishable, at least, while the latter was the agent for a

---

[1] We must remember that, even in his suicidal despair, the worth of Juliet and the worth of his love for her remain intact in the mind of Romeo, are even enhanced.

poetry of romantic love. The *Sonnets*, whether early or late, and the poetry of the romantic lovers, speak in a personal voice (a voice original to Shakespeare and which he developed within himself), but the speech of low comic characters was conceived as being uttered through throats other than the poet's. What they uttered was selectively echoed, and the principle of selection was probably that of adaptation to the vocal capacities of the comic actors. It was next suggested, after the introduction of these external voices, that Shakespeare gradually assimilated the vocabulary[1]—and therewith the rhythms and the tones—of these external voices into his 'serious' verse. We must include their grammatical inflexions: for, to put it shortly, whereas the Shakespearean Romantic Lover lives for his future so that the grammatical form of the verb he uses tends to be the Future Conditional—expressive of his desire—the chosen verb forms of the Comic Character, by contrast, reflect his absorption in a present actuality. But, in incorporating these elements into his serious verse, Shakespeare extended the bounds of his personal voice. What he came to include as part of himself became part of the vocal agent by which he expressed that self.

Even so this must be modified. Shakespeare's experience increased in time beyond his own limits to utter. Though his own voice presumably developed and deepened, in common with those of other men 'passing through nature to eternity', what he conceived outgrew his power to say.[2] Hence he depended, for poetic life and for livelihood, on surrogates.[3] The limits to what he could say in his own voice are perhaps discoverable in the latest sonnets. After the latest sonnets he spoke through the vocal organs of Burbage and others.

Consequently, it is hard to attach enough importance to the early low comic characters once it is conceded that, but for the Nurse in *Romeo and Juliet*, we would hardly have got Falstaff, and that but for Falstaff, with his prose speeches full of the stuff of

---

[1] See F. P. Wilson: *Shakespeare and the Diction of Common Life.*

[2] Shakespeare's last known appearance as an actor was in 1603 in Jonson's *Sejanus.* See E. K. Chambers, Vol. II, p. 367.

[3] This might seem less tendentious when it is recollected that no living actor today could be expected to effectively play, or even speak, more than a small proportion of the parts created by Shakespeare. Then how could Shakespeare? Contrast Shakespeare with Tennyson, the prisoner of his voice.

common life,[1] we would hardly have got the verse soliloquies of Hamlet which are also full of the stuff of common life. Neither would we have had those sonnets, occurring about three-quarters of the way through the series, which differ from the early sonnets in being full of the stuff of common life—with all its linguistic, grammatical and vocal implications. This, then, is a first finding in our response to Shakespeare's development: a widening of experience through the surrender of a personal voice to the heard voices of others.

Also to be borne in mind is the dismantling of The Theatre in 1598. It had been opened in 1576, and it is hard not to believe that the experience of twenty-two years playing there had not convinced producers and actors that it could be improved upon. The materials of The Theatre were carried over London Bridge and included in The Globe (which opened in 1599 with *Henry V*), but it is fair to suppose that the new theatre embodied structural changes in the light of that long experience. It is probable that the structural features of The Theatre which had satisfied everyone for over a generation were repeated in The Globe, but that those things in The Theatre which had annoyed everyone were carefully avoided in The Globe. The Lord Chamberlain's Men were not moving into another house which had already been built, having to make the best of it. On the contrary, The Globe was carefully built to their own specifications in the light of their long experience of The Theatre, of its shortcomings and of its merits. It is sane to suppose, too, that The Globe was also larger than The Theatre, for the Chamberlain's Men were the leading firm in a boom industry.

Now how much knowledge of the applied science of acoustics the late Elizabethans had cannot be determined. But this much is certain: no two buildings, then or now, could have the same acoustics. The acoustics of The Globe, if that building differed in the minutest degree in shape or size from The Theatre, and it was probably different in both respects, were different from the acoustics of The Theatre. This is relevant because The Globe opened with *Henry V*, and it is obvious that this play is, among

[1] We cannot be unmindful here of the stimulus exerted by *Every Man in his Humour* (1597), the stimulus exerted by Jonson's own voice as well as the voices of his London creatures. Shakespeare's name appears in the cast list of this play.

other things, a deliberate trial of unknown acoustic properties. The Choruses or Henry's 'Once more unto the Breach, / Deare friends, once more' test these properties in one respect, viz: the capacities of the new theatre to take and fling back clarion tones—high-pitched, strong and ringing sounds, expressive of young confidence. Then the *sotto voce* exchanges of Henry and the common soldiers, Bates, Court, Williams, before Agincourt, and his prayer before that battle, test those properties in another respect: the capacity of the new theatre to so hold spoken sound that a speech uttered in quiet but deep tones could be heard throughout. In the light of Shakespeare's plays following *Henry V*, it would seem that The Globe passed the second test magnificently, but was less successful in the first.

Now what may seem pure conjecture has this support: only after *Henry V* do we find in Shakespeare a thorough employment of *sotto voce*. There are, of course, soliloquies before *Henry V*, but these are more in the nature of addresses *to* the audience than musings assumed to be overheard *by* the audience. But for The Globe, *Hamlet* (the 1603 Quarto minus the soliloquies remains a problem) might not have been conceived for want of acoustics capable of conveying those parts of Hamlet's soliloquies which are nearly whispered. But The Globe, as an auditorium, became assured to Shakespeare; and, when its capacities became known, the sounds of *Hamlet* were imaginatively heard in that setting in the act of composition. And not only *Hamlet*. On the other hand, the response of The Globe to shouted speech at a certain pitch and volume, above a certain volume, seems to have been poor. The Theatre had been excellent for this—witness the opening speech of *I Henry VI*,[1] and many other speeches in the early Chronicle plays of Shakespeare (let alone, perhaps, *Tamberlaine*)—but The Globe's walls refracted or muffled. Hence, no vaunters after Henry V shout at his pitch. There are indeed vaunters after Henry V. Coriolanus

---

[1] Hung be the heavens with black, yield day to night;
Comets importing change of Times and States,
Brandish your crystall Tresses in the Skie,
And with them scourge the bad revolting Stars,
That have consented unto *Henries* death . . .

(I, i, 1–5.)

is one: but he declaims, though as loudly, in a harder voice at a lower level in the scale. Harder because, unlike Henry V, he is not happy or thrilled. Other loud speakers after Henry V are Othello, Macbeth, Lear, Timon, Antony, Leontes. But the Globe was not distorting or unresponsive to the voices of anger and passion. Provided the voices of anger and passion avoided clarion tones—which these angry and passionate men do avoid—The Globe *played*. Again conjecture: but the question of acoustics is inextricably involved with another consideration—the one to which we alluded at the opening of this section.

For we must also bear in mind that Shakespeare and his 'fellows' were alike ageing, and that, in the process of ageing, all men's voices alter. They say, and wish to say, other things than they said in their youth, for what is said is coloured by the saying. Shakespeare's physical voice, on the evidence of the later sonnets, altered. In the main it deepened and took on a harsher edge. But so did the voices of Burbage and the others. Burbage, for instance, who possibly played Romeo, years later probably played 'young Hamlet', later still 'greued Othello', and after that 'kind Leir'. The voice (and figure) of Burbage had, with the passing of time, become unfit to speak Romeo's lines, but had become an instrument apt for the lines of the tragic heroes. Such possibilities and probabilities are not often mentioned in Shakespeare criticism, if at all. But the known voices of his instruments, of his 'fellows', must have been Shakespeare's habitual consideration in the creation of his plays. There were also the voices of the prentice players between 1600 and 1611 which might have elicited of Shakespeare not only interest and involuntary affection but also poignant memories of their predecessors. But enough of this. Omitting the Lover in the Golden Comedies (whose voice is fuller than is that of the Lover in the Early Comedies) and *Troilus* (where Shakespeare has to remember himself, though, I dare say, a connection here with the 'story' of the *Sonnets* is clear enough), let us consider the voice of Othello as a contrast to the voice of the Romantic Lover of the earliest comedies or *Romeo and Juliet*.

vii

Othello, like the young men in the Romantic Comedies, is a lover. But, whereas the early lover beheld his mistress romantically, Othello preferred to be beheld romantically by his mistress. He saw to it that Desdemona regarded him as a romantic figure whenever he related to her his life-story which was, we are told, often. Whether the audience also regard him as a romantic figure, as he indulges in his autobiographical reminiscences (no other Shakespearian personage is so given to this form of egoism), depends on whether we accept him at his own valuation.

Othello, like Romeo romantic but not romantic in Romeo's style, is—unlike Romeo—not young. Iago alludes to him as 'an olde blacke Ram' (I, i). Othello, less rudely, says of himself that his youthful 'heat' is 'defunct' (I, iii). He admits elsewhere that he is 'declin'd Into the vale of yeares' (III, iii), to which he adds parenthetically 'yet that's not much'—meaning not so much 'declin'd' 'as all that'. Not so much, but enough to have given him a past, to have furnished him with memories, to have made him experienced.

Because of this 'decline'—this past, this experience—his voice is not like Romeo's any more than his love is like Romeo's. Romeo's voice, until his state of despair, like the voices of the other early young romantic lovers, is—as we have noted—eager, soft in timbre, high in pitch. Romeo *aspires* to Juliet, poised above him on a balcony; and the other young lovers see—or put —their mistresses 'on a pedestal', an apt figure to describe their lovers' psychological and vocal approach. Romeo has little or no history, though the 'houses' of the Montagues and Capulets have, and he only looks forward to the consummation of his love. His speeches are prayers that his wishes may be granted; and their structural tense is therefore an Indicative Present tending to a Conditional Future. Youth and desire determine the cast and modulation of his voice.

But Othello's nature, conditioned by his years (or experience), and his kind of love (he less aspired to Desdemona than demanded her pity, admiration and regard—which she duly gave), and determined by his race or colour, requires for its vocal correlate and expression a massive and rolling bass. That this is generally accepted is suggested by stage tradition. No theatrical producer would choose a man—for no audience would accept such a man—with a thin, high, or even a normal tenor voice, for the part of Othello.[1]

Now the stage tradition that Othello should have a deep and resonant voice has the soundest justification. It is this: the language attributed to Othello in the printed text *can* only be uttered—effectively uttered, uttered so as not to sound absurd—in a deep and rolling voice. As Milton's voice can be heard behind (or through) the printed text of *Paradise Lost*, so can Othello's voice be heard behind (or through) the printed speeches allotted to him; but the latter is a dramatic voice, and Othello's voice is not Shakespeare's.

In a famous essay, 'The *Othello* Music',[2] G. Wilson Knight described and defined the poetry of this play which, as he said, is 'dominated by [that of] its protagonist'. Knight quotes the lines:

> had she bin true,
> If Heaven would make me such another world
> Of one entire and perfect chrysolite,
> I'd not have sold her for it.

> (V, ii, 143–146)

and remarks that in Othello's poetry the images are 'concrete, detached; seen, but not apprehended'.[3] He also notes Othello's proneness towards 'the long comparison, explicitly made, where in *King Lear* or *Macbeth* a series of swiftly evolving metaphors would be more characteristic'. As an illustration he adduces:

> Like to the Ponticke Sea,
> Whose Icie Current, and compulsive course,
> Nev'r keepes retyring ebbe, but deepes due on
> To the Proponticke, and the Hellespont:

---

[1] In practice, of course, producers have to make do with what they have got when a Paul Robeson is not available. But an actor, whose natural voice is of merely medium pitch, instinctively deepens it when he assumes the rôle of Othello.

[2] *The Wheel of Fire*, 4th ed. (Methuen, 1949), pp. 97–117.

[3] *Ibid.*, p. 99, whereas in *Macbeth* the images are 'continually vague, mastered by passion; apprehended, but not seen'.

Even so my bloody thoughts, with violent pace
Shall nev'r looke backe, nev'r ebbe to humble Love
Till that a capeable, and wide Revenge
Swallow them up. Now by yond Marble Heaven,
In the due reverence of a Sacred vow,
I heere engage my words.

(III, iii, 453-462)

and suggests that it is a sign of Iago's success when at last
Othello descends from this noble and rounded speech and falls
into 'incoherent mutterings'.[1] Othello does of course regain his
imposing presence and demeanour, his marmoreal speech, at the
end. The breakdown is in Act III, sc. iii and in Act IV, sc. i.

To this account of Othello's poetry (and the title, 'The *Othello*
Music', obviously emphasizes the sound of the poetry), one
wishes to add here observations on the kind of voice required
for its effective, and only proper, delivery aloud.

Instancing the quotations given above, or instancing the
speech before the Senate, beginning:

Most Potent, Grave, and Reveren'd Signiors . . .

(I, iii, 76)

or instancing his final address, beginning:

Soft you: a word or two before you goe . . .

(V, ii, 338)

we say that Othello is assuming an audience. It is an audience
to be impressed, however 'rude' he is in his speech.[2] What happens when there is no actual and ready-to-be-impressed audience of senators or officials? When there's an audience consist-
ting of only one—namely Iago? When this happens he *creates*
an audience so that 'yond Marble Heaven' is impressed into
listening too. *Othello* is a domestic tragedy, but even in the bed-
room (and Desdemona cannot hear for she is asleep) Othello
yet summons an audience of 'Chaste Starres' and frames his
words—and so their delivery—accordingly.

---

[1] *The Wheel of Fire*, 4th ed. (Methuen, 1949), p. 117.

[2] Rude am I, in my speech,
And little bless'd with the soft phrase of Peace. . . .

(I, iii, 81, 82.)

This is good gamesmanship to be compared with Mark Antony's protesta-
tion, 'I am no Orator', *Julius Caesar*, III, ii.

For the words control the delivery. The phonetic constitu-
ents of the words of the speeches of Othello compel a slow massive
orotund delivery. Othello uses the long—central or back, open
or half-open—vowels and diphthongs and especially the long
sound of the letter o [ou], as in 'Potent', 'Proponticke', 'chryso-
lite', in extraordinary numbers, and the high (or 'light', short
and close) vowels—those making for rapid utterance—are
correspondingly few. But other factors compel a grand, a slow,
a resounding delivery. First, there is his habit of speaking, as it
were, from a platform to a wondering audience. When Othello
engages 'Heaven' and when, in fact, there is but a single
human listener, Iago, to take note:

> Now by yond Marble Heaven,
> In the due reverence of a Sacred vow,
> I heere engage my words.[1]

then a large hall for the hearing is assumed, cased by a 'Marble
Heaven', a roof that must resound. Moreover, a solemn address
from the place of honour in a large hall must be delivered at a
slower pace than a private conversation. It must also be delivered more loudly than a private conversation—and delivered
standing. Until he falls full-length on the stage, foaming at the
mouth, Othello must always stand: the heroic posture must fit
the heroic words. The bold but simple syntax, the lucid concrete imagery, the punctuation—as given in the Folio and the
Quarto—which exists as much for absorption of resonance as to
point grammatical relation,[2] all assist and force the actor to
give a majestic and orotund delivery.

Othello's voice owes its depth and resonance partly to his

---

[1] The hemistich consists of a spondee ('Now by'), followed by a spondee
('yond Mar'), followed by an iambic ('-ble Heav-'), followed by a feminine
ending ('-on'). Suppose the first two syllables reversed ('By now'), and the
hemistich becomes easy to read rapidly. But, in Othello's order the syllables
'by' and 'Mar' have perforce to be given an extraordinary stress and
length.

[2] For example, in:

> Most Potent, Grave, and Reveren'd Signiors . . .

the comma after 'Grave' is grammatically redundant, but the 'a' of Grave,
naturally long, has been lengthened, as the initial capital denotes, and a
pause is necessary for absorption of resonance in the Senate Chamber as
well as for the sake of impressiveness.

maturity (compared with Romeo he is old) and partly to the nature of his love, this last being, as we have seen, closely determined by the romantic manner with which he beholds himself. But Othello's voice is not only his own: it is also the voice of an ethnic group.

We have all heard the magnificent negro voice as exemplified by Paul Robeson. Compared with the European voice it is full, deep and rolling,[1] and there is available a precise anatomical explanation for its superb quality. It is permissible, even reasonable, to suppose that Shakespeare had heard, say, a Nubian (whether a Moor or not, Othello we are told, is 'black' and 'sooty') speak with such a voice and, in speaking, boast. For such voices, with their ample swell, are genetically better adapted to expansive boasting than to rapid conversation. But while we are on this subject we had better touch on the voice of the Prince of Morocco in *The Merchant of Venice*.

For the resemblance: Morocco, in his self-description,[2] like Othello, boasts of his martial achievements and their history. They both boast in long, colourful, admiration-demanding and magnificent speeches. For the difference: despite the impressiveness of Morocco's opening:

> Mislike me not for my complexion,
> The shadowed liverie of the burnisht sunne,
> To whom I am a neighbour, and neere bred . . .

he cannot keep it up.

His voice at the outset is measured and impressive but, as his second speech nears to a conclusion, his voice lightens and quickens, and on his next appearance (*Merchant of Venice*, II, vii) it never reaches the depth of pitch, the richness of tone or

---

[1] A *minority* of Negroes (West African, West Indian, American) have not deep and rolling voices but eunuchoid and whining. We hear them as good-natured and obsequious railroad-car attendants, etc., in American films. I am inclined to think that those who whine up the scale in the words 'Ya-as Saah, me too tink . . .', etc., have either cultivated a falsetto in the belief that a white employer likes to hear this voice from a servant (thus not putting to shame the voice of the employer), or that they are genetically descended from a tribe different from those who possess deep and rolling voices. We must remember that the ethnography of black Africa is as varied as Europe, and that African voices, whether in Africa or the New World, reflect this variegation.

[2] *Merchant of Venice*, II, i, 1–3.

the degree of resonance of his opening address. His voice has a striking general resemblance to Othello's, but from the beginning was a baritone to Othello's bass, and it ends by becoming thin, fevered and almost high-pitched. From this one can infer some conclusions concerning Shakespeare's own voice, his own power of hearing and that of the actor who first played Othello.

Troilus was the last young Romantic Lover (agreed that Troilus was disabused of his 'romantic' love) with whom Shakespeare shared his own voice, or lent it from memory. The last: for Claudio in *Measure for Measure* and Hamlet are not primarily lovers. The first is an object in a condemned cell, the second had other matters beside a one-time mistress to fuss about. Troilus is the last, for Antony is on in years, even older than Othello, and, when we come to Florizel and Ferdinand, we find that Shakespeare is not giving *his* contemporary voice to them (Shakespeare's contemporary voice is occupying rather Leontes and Prospero who, in *The Winter's Tale* and *The Tempest* respectively, are the central voices), but rather remembering his early voice (now long past) and memorially attributing it to prospective and menacing sons-in-law.

Othello was the first of the two middle-aged lovers; the other was Antony. Now, although Shakespeare could conceive the later sonnets (or even Hamlet, even Iago) in terms of his own voice, yet Othello's great negro voice was something outside his own vocal resources. But he may have *heard* that voice outside himself, heard its prototype and then echoed it, just as he *heard* and echoed the voices of the prototypes of his low comic characters.

We are told, on a measure of early authority, that Burbage played 'greued Othello'. Burbage had played the early Richard III and perhaps had played Romeo. But over the course of years one is quite fairly obliged to suppose that Burbage's voice (and his figure, and his appearance, and his personality) had changed, or developed, had lost some capacities and acquired others—as did other men's voices including Shakespeare's.[1] One can also fairly suppose that Burbage's voice changed like

[1] The date of Richard Burbage's birth is unknown. He was junior to his brother, Cuthbert, who was born in 1566/7, but had been long established as an actor by 1594. He died in 1619. See E. K. Chambers, *The Elizabethan Stage*, Vol. II, p. 307.

other men's: that it lost its top notes, became fuller, grew harsher in timbre, gained in expressiveness and strength, became more of an instrument to control at will, became capable of reflecting experience, and deepened in its pitch norm.

'*Othello* is dominated by its protagonist.'[1] That is surely so, but the great tragedies that follow—*Macbeth, King Lear, Timon, Coriolanus, Antony and Cleopatra*—are hardly less dominated by *their* protagonists. From *Othello* to *Antony and Cleopatra*—and beyond, for there are Pericles, Leontes and Prospero—we have a series of plays in each of which there is a figure, or—better—a voice, differentiated from the other figures or voices in the plays in which they occur. They are the central voices in the multi-voiced plays in which they occur, differentiated more decisively than any one voice had been differentiated from its respective vocal context in the twenty-three or so plays preceding *Hamlet* and *Othello*. Othello, and the other characters whose names provide the titles of the plays that follow (and then Leontes and then Prospero), are not simply just the heroes of their plays, as was Romeo in his play, nor even, simply, in the Henry Jamesian term, 'central intelligences', but 'central voices'. Shakespeare seems to have invested in Othello, Macbeth, Lear and the others, the greatest part of himself. Consequently audiences and readers invest more of themselves in these figures than they ever did in the heroes or near-heroes of the early plays. In the earlier plays Shakespeare does not especially speak through one person but diffuses his voice among all. Othello and the others are the sentient centres of the plays in which they occur. We could say that they are the dramatic surrogates for Shakespeare.

Surrogates. It is our belief that Shakespeare's exploration of experience through the medium of vocal sound (accompanied, certainly, by the visible movement of bodies on a stage) developed far beyond the capacities of his own voice as an agent to transmit. Many poets are contained by their own voices, compose within the limits of their own voices, are perhaps possessed by their own voices. What applies to other poets would seem to have applied to Shakespeare (with the exception of the 'low' comic persons) in his earlier plays. But he came, gradually, not to be confined by his own voice but to possess voices not his

[1] G. Wilson Knight, *op. cit.*, see p. 210 above.

own. These outside voices became instruments (and what is an instrument but a surrogate for an agent, as the tool is for the hand?) and superior to the agent for a special purpose (as the screw-driver can drive a screw far more effectively than the hand which holds the driver). Shakespeare must have explored and exploited one (there were others, but especially there was one) of his career-long fellows as a surrogate voice, as an instrument. This fellow-player (if he had died earlier, or had never existed, what might have happened?), probably Richard Burbage, had the command of a voice which Shakespeare came to employ for a series of tragic explorations of experience which, rendered in sound, was beyond his own power to utter. Through this surrogate or funnel he directed imagined vocal harmonies of a complexity beyond the complexity of the later sonnets. The enormous extension of verbal possibilities which Shakespeare apprehended, but could not say, were conceived with close reference to this surrogate and on an imaginative habitation of his being. 'Kind Leir' was perhaps at least twice as old as Burbage in 1606, but not older than Shakespeare felt, and no man of eighty could play Lear.

This is not to conclude however that Shakespeare, from *Othello* onwards, entered entirely into the person of Burbage-Othello, Burbage-Macbeth, etc., to the exclusion of all others. The possession of a main instrument led to a subsidiary control and command over a dozen or score of others—just as, say, a man who attains a mastery of a mechanical skill gains an insight into other related skills. Anyone can recognize not only Othello's voice behind the printed signs but also Iago's, even Brabantio's. *Through*, and only through, complete mastery of one instrument, the poet gained competence in the management of an orchestra.

Whatever the measure of sympathy the reader may feel inclined to give to the 'theory' of this argument, he will feel that much depends on conjecture—however sensible, even obvious, that conjecture may be. But one has been limited to a short essay on a subject that requires not one book but many for its development. But our present purpose is limited to the pointing of a major contrast between those who are primarily great 'I' poets, like Tennyson, Shelley and Milton, whom we considered in an earlier section, and a great poetic dramatist.

VIII The Voice of Marlowe

i

SHAKESPEARE was a dramatist. Marlowe was a dramatist. They were both poets. The statements pass but cause discomfort. The discomfort is provoked by the word 'dramatist', only dependently by the word 'poets'. When we say 'dramatist', our imaginations turn to 'scene' and to plural invented voices issuing from bodies occupying that scene. As for 'poet', our imagination turns to men uttering words in their own voices. The discomfort arises, I suggest, from a suspicion that if Shakespeare and Marlowe were both dramatists then they belonged to two different kinds of dramatist. If so, they also belonged to two different kinds of poet.

One more statement: they were both born in the same year, 1564. That is unexceptionable, but yet in a way misleads. Marlowe had done, or was done for, before Shakespeare had scarcely got going. Hence it is usual to treat of Marlowe in the manuals of literary history first, as a precursor. Yet by reversing the order we perhaps come to perceive more clearly the essential nature of each man, to understand there is dramatist and dramatist, and poet and poet—to appreciate the better the differences between poetic dramatist and dramatic poet.

Long ago, in 1918, T. S. Eliot published his essay on Marlowe. In that essay the word 'tone' occurs, I believe, more frequently than in any other essay of comparable length either by this or by any other critic. Thus, for example, of the *Jew of Malta* we read: '. . . if we attend with a careful ear to the versification, we find that Marlowe develops a tone to suit this force, and even perhaps that the tone is his most powerful and mature tone.'

And of *Dr Faustus*: 'In *Faustus* Marlowe went further: he broke
up the line, to a gain in intensity, in the last soliloquy; and he
developed a new and important conversational tone in the
dialogue of Faustus with the devil.'[1]

Tone. Now by 'tone' is surely meant a particular inflexion,
heard by the inner ear, of a physical voice—Marlowe's. My
suggestion is that Marlowe never inhabited the voices of the
players as Shakespeare did (perhaps because for Marlowe these
were 'the' players and not 'his' players), subordinated his own
voice to them so as to use them in their variety. Nevertheless,
Marlowe's own voice certainly changed in the course of the
few years—five or six—between the beginning of his dramatic
career and his death in 1593.

ii

To 1587–88 *Tamburlaine* Parts I and II are attributed, and
here more magnificently than anywhere, is the insistent, mono-
tonous, in its strict sense of one-toned, Marlovian voice. Marlowe here could not have been what he *is*, with all his out-
rageously challenging *panache*, had he not been one-toned. For
only by 'harping on one note' is the pressing nature of a defiant
and manic need to challenge communicated. In illustrating one
cannot do better than quote the lines already best known, if
only because the following description of that voice will then
the more easily be tested by the reader who can relate the description to lines which he will have surely heard in the inner
ear, uttered by their author:

> The thirst of raigne and sweetnes of a crown,
> That causde the eldest sonne of heauenly *Ops*,
> To thrust his doting father from his chaire,
> And place himselfe in the Emperiall heauen,
> Moou'd me to manage armes against thy state.
> What better president than mightie *Ioue*?
> Nature that fram'd vs of foure Elements,

---

[1] T. S. Eliot: 'Christopher Marlowe', *Selected Essays* (Faber, 1932),
pp. 122, 123.

Ibid., pp. 122, 123. Mr. Eliot's essay antedated the bibliographical dis-
coveries of W. W. Greg, the effect of which is to place *Dr. Faustus* at the end
of Marlowe's brief career and not between *Tamburlaine* and the *Jew of Malta*.

Warring within our breasts for regiment,
Doth teach vs all to haue aspyring minds:
Our soules, whose faculties can comprehend
The wondrous Archtitecture of the world:
And measure euery wandring plannets course,
Still climing after knowledge infinite,
And alwaies moouing as the restles Spheares,
Wils vs to weare our selues and neuer rest,
Vntill we reach the ripest fruit of all,
That perfect blisse and sole felicities,
The sweet fruition of an earthly crowne.[1]

Marlowe's early voice is a voice that is declaiming, and declaiming at one particular pitch. This could be separately (separately from the act of 'hearing' by a sympathetic reader) inferred from the knowledge that the lines were delivered from the centre of Henslowe's first theatre before a turbulent audience, and that the acoustics of that theatre, like the first structure of the brothers Burbage, required an actor to shout to be heard; or it could be inferred from the reputation of Alleyn's style of playing, or from the echo—as late as 1598—of his playing, and of Marlowe's voice, in the mouth of Pistol in 2 *Henry IV* with his 'hollow-pampered Jades of Asia' (II, iv, 178); or inferred from the knowledge that this was the accepted tragic style of playing ('Ercles vaine, a tyrants vaine') to 'Split the eares of the Groundlings' in the early theatres—the theatres before The Globe was built and whose acoustic properties permitted a Hamlet to speak *sotto voce* and be audible.

The accepted declamatory style. It could be inferred that it was the accepted style because the phonic properties of Seneca's Latin demanded such a style for their oration. Moreover we can hear Marlowe's shouted voice feebly imitated by Greene in his *Alphonsus* and by Peele in his *Battle of Alcazar*. Their imitation is feeble because it is evident that the situations and histories of the heroes of Peele and Greene required of them that they vaunt with 'high, astounding terms', but it is equally evident—to limit ourselves to Peele—that though the poet of *David and Bethsabe* had a musical, seductive voice (physical voice), capable of a kind of a high humming incantatory note, it was incapable of

---

[1] *The Works of Christopher Marlowe*, edited by C. F. Tucker Brooke (O.U.P., 2nd imp., 1929), p. 32.

Marlowe's driven, taut, yet magnificent, harshness. Therefore, though the speeches of Peele's conquering hero require to be hurled with vigour, they cannot be so hurled because Peele's own voice (though it strove to imitate Marlowe's) was incapable of attaining the gritted edge. Consequently, the phonic properties of Peele's language resist the actor's attempt to deliver it to suit the martial savageries the scenario calls on him to perform. What is remarkable about Marlowe is that even such words as 'ripest fruit', 'blisses' and 'sweet' (in isolation they are soft and Keatsian words) are included in the shouting.

Marlowe, through the vocal organs of Edward Alleyn, is of course—not plainly shouting (nor 'ranting' which disguises the nature of the delivery under a term denotative of printed style) which is to reduce all things to a common loudness and a hoarse violence—declaiming, and declaiming at a specialized pitch which has none of the disadvantages of shouting (e.g. a uniformity of stress so that nothing has been gained except the release of anger), and is almost sung out at one register above. He is certainly declaiming thus—for Tamburlaine is not *confessing* to his audience from a position down-stage—the motive of his thrust for power. Tamburlaine-Marlowe is mid- or upstage in one of the first public theatres and his vaunting, his manifesto, is attended to by his three disciples whose attitude is a 'hear, hear!' Since Marlowe is in the person of his protagonist nothing in the nature of a genuine counter-argument—which would have been dramatic—can be expected. Except in the final doom of the protagonists as peremptorily *shown* (but not, with the possible exception of Edward II, really *said*) in the conclusion of his plays, no dissent from the hero's premises can be granted. Thus Theridamus, one of the disciples, simply confirms in the same style and in the same timbre. If *his* voice is less robust, it is only because his energy supports, adds what was left out, but does not originate. The other two auditors of Tamburlaine similarly echo him:

> And that made me to joine with *Tamburlain*,
> For he is grosse and like the massie earth,
> That mooues no vpwards, nor by princely deeds
> Doth meane to soare aboue the highest sort.[1]

[1] *Op. cit.*, p. 32.

Tamburlaine is declaiming, and they are all declaiming, as indeed their tactical relation to each other in the scene required, and as the nature of the acoustics of this early theatre and the Senecan tradition demanded.

If you are to roar or vaunt, you must alter register as a car changes gear, and risk hoarseness rather than shrillness. Marlowe's voice is energetic, savage, harsh, of a ruthless and even pace, curiously unvarying (Shakespeare came to vary as soon as he perceived the effectiveness of his instruments) in pitch, pace or volume. Above all it is energetic and avoids the shrillness endemic to Shelley despite its imagery of aspiration. It fits the violent and barbarous acts. It is true, as Wolfgang Clemen points out, that Marlowe's text seethes with such verbs as 'mount', 'climb', 'soar' and 'rise'.[1] But though that makes him agree with Shelley in the area of vocabulary which of all parts of speech is most revealing (a man reveals, if not his actions, then his intentions or unactable desires by the verbs he employs), it does not follow that Marlowe's voice was like Shelley's, or that an actor of Marlowe should speak as a reciter of Shelley.

On the contrary, despite the dazzling heights, the climbing, the soaring, the hyperboles like 'topless', the 'over-reaching' as Harry Levin (borrowing a phrase from the Tudor grammarians) terms it in his stimulating study,[2] Marlowe's voice is altogether different from Shelley's, quite apart from the fact that Shelley's screeching—though painfully penetrative in Hogg's rooms at University College, Oxford in 1810—would never have been heard in Henslowe's open-to-the-air structure in 1587. The imagery of both poets is one of rising and soaring, but Shelley soars so as to keep on moving forward; Marlowe (or Tamburlaine who is at least most of Marlowe) soars to gain a station of dominance from which he may trample. True, it lay only in *wish* as translated into the action of plays and not in the action of life, and however Marlowe vaunted and threatened in plays he probably trampled on nobody. But the patterns of wish are operative where poetry is concerned. In life wishes, unless and until they are translated into action, are harmless and only God can call to account the wisher after he is dead; but in poetry, expressions of wish are as potent and operative as facts

[1] In *Shakespeare's Bilder* (Bonn, 1936), p. 334.
[2] See *The Overreacher: a study of Christopher Marlowe* (Faber, 1954).

and deeds in life, or more so. If this seems too easy, let us remember that poetry is a part of life, and for some the major, even the decisive, part.

Marlowe's soaring Tamburlaine is unlike Shelley's soaring lark because Tamburlaine is ready to cut off heads on his way up to the top and, having got to the top, is ready presumably to descend and to sit satisfied. Certainly the 'earthly' crown is a jab against ancestral Christian striving for a heavenly one, but the result of the exchange is to be presented with one of Shelley's tyrants. But Marlowe-Tamburlaine's longing is intensely metaphysical, and that is enough to distinguish him from practical machiaevels, like Shakespeare's Richard III, whose ambitions are strictly mundane. Tamburlaine wants a mundane crown, but its capture would mark the satisfaction of a metaphysical, limitless thirst and so is paradoxical. But the fact that Tamburlaine's aim is a terrestial, and not—as in Marlowe's father's time—a celestial, one is precisely what gives the grinding and harsh (and yet thrilled) edge to his voice.

Marlowe-Tamburlaine and Shelley both aspire, but whereas the former (in the realm of wish which is real in poetry) would 'wade through slaughter to a throne', Shelley's lark wouldst hardly hurt a fly or whatever the lark's legitimate, because natural, prey is. Moreover Shelley's lark could never be satisfied and so stay still, however high it got, and though it, too, has to descend, Shelley leaves that unsaid. He would not have been Shelley if he had remembered that or made much of the descent. Marlowe's Tamburlaine can only reach his summit (paradoxically, by returning to squat on the ground with a crown about his temples) by executing, chopping up, squashing and killing all or everyone else that inhabits the earth except willing slaves or echoing supporters like Theridamus. Again, this is only in the wish. But what the wish involves for the saying of the poetry is the timbre of iron determination and not the breathy shrillness of Shelley, for even though the imagery belongs to the same category it is owned by a different temperament and aimed at a contrasting target.

For the early poetry requires for its saying, whatever the aesthetic excellence and delight of such hard and dizzy heights as

> *Zenocrate*, louelier than the Loue of *Ioue*,
> Brighter than is the siluer Rhodope,

(wherein Rhodope is envisaged as high up and as glitteringly artificial, rather than as flowing river), a ruthless, bloody harshness. Plenty of such images as that of Bajazeth in his cage dashing out his brains against the bars must act as pictorial cartoons demonstrating that wish. Since that wish is genuine the illustrations are not shown ironically. Not the brutality, nor yet the absurdity, of that wish are known by Marlowe before the results of his experiment are brought in. If the wish is eventually changed, rather than withdrawn, it is because experience disappoints. The hero find reality inferior to the infinitude of wish.

Of course the passage first quoted, no less than Tamburlaine's apostrophe to Zenocrate, is lyrical. While these particular passages are uttered there are no cartoons to amaze the eye, but these will follow as consequences of Tamburlaine's postulates. What is remarkable is that Marlowe, who had evidently heard Spenser's voice (heard Spenser's voice in *The Faerie Queene*, if not from his person), could transform that slow, gentle and musing voice into sound so rapid, martial and stirring. Spenser and Marlowe! How different their voices! and yet, as J. M. Robertson first noted, Marlowe stole, on an occasion, from Spenser. But if the lines Marlowe stole are listened to not in isolation but in the context of Tamburlaine's whole speech (and likewise the lines of Spenser are listened to in relation to the preceding stanza), the measure of Marlowe's act of transformation can be better appraised than by a brief inspection of a parallel passage.[1]

Here are Spenser's stanzas:

> His haughtie helmet, horrid all with gold,
>   Both glorious brightnesse, and great terrour bred;
>   For all the crest a Dragon did enfold
>   With greedie pawes, and ouer all did spred
>   His golden wings: his dreadfull hideous hed
>   Close couched on the beuer, seem'd to throw
>   From flaming mouth bright sparkles fierie red,
>   That suddeine horror to faint harts did show;
> And scaly tayle was stretcht adowne his backe full low.

[1] The bare presentation of the parallel is all that the economy of space presumably allowed Mr Eliot to offer in his essay on Marlowe.

Vpon the top of all his loftie crest,
  A bunch of haires discolourd diuersly,
  With sprincled pearle, and gold full richly drest,
  Did shake, and seem'd to daunce for iollity,
  Like to an Almond tree ymounted hye
  On top of greene *Selinis* all alone,
  With blossomes braue bedecked daintily;
  Whose tender locks do tremble euery one
At euery little breath, that vnder heauen is blowne.[1]

And here is the speech from Marlowe incorporating these stolen lines about the almond tree:

  Thorow the streets with troops of conquered kings,
  Ile ride in golden armour like the Sun,
  And in my helme a triple plume shal spring,
  Spangled with Diamonds dancing in the aire,
  To note me Emperour of the three fold world,
  Like to an almond tree ymounted high,
  Vpon the lofty and celestiall mount,
  Of euer greene *Selinus* queintly dect
  With bloomes more white than *Hericinas* browes,
  Whose tender blossoms tremble euery one,
  At euery little breath that thorow heauen is blowen:
  Then in my coach like *Saturnes* royal son,
  Mounted his shining chariot, gilt with fire,
  And drawen with princely Eagles through the path,
  Pau'd with bright Christall, and enchac'd with starres,
  When all the Gods stand gazing at his pomp,
  So will I ride through *Samarcanda* streets,
  Vntil my soule disseuered from this flesh,
  Shall mount the milk-white way and meet him there.[2]

Although Spenser's subject is ostensibly the bracing and masculine one of a vigorous knight on horseback approaching the spectator, his movement is slowed to a standstill while his helmet, crest, arms and accoutrements are described. No one can say that the description is urgent or lively. There is a dreamy lassitude about the pictures. It is not that the disparity between a vigorous and stern subject and a leisured and slow voice is a

---

[1] *The Faerie Queene*, I, vii, 31–32.
[2] *2 Tamburlaine*, IV. 4. 4093–4 III.

fault. On the contrary, the slow and leisured voice is necessary for preserving the mood of enchantment in which *The Faerie Queene* is conducted. By 'mood of enchantment' we point as much to a linguistic, specifically grammatic, method (demanding for its rendering aloud a certain kind of voice) as to a state of emotion. Spenser's verbs are here Present and Indicative and Active, verbs which normally create a sense of exciting events now happening, of men and objects in strenuous, vivid and immediate movement. They do not so here. The whole scene is distanced, put into that remote perspective without light or shade proper to Romance, by the use of the word 'seem'd' (as much as to say: Fancied, put outside the laws of time and space, none of this happening really); by the absence of metrical or semantic stress on the verbs because of their position in the build of the line and the build of the sentences; by the length and construction of the sentence which conveys a muffled and hazy effect instead of sharp definition;[1] and by the liberal sprinkling of generalizing adjectives. There is also that alexandrine which, as has often been observed, prevents Spenser from ever gathering any real speed—or, it should be added, vocal force.

But turning to Marlowe, we find that before the line about the 'Almond tree' is reached, the speaker is in a state of high euphoria. It cannot be reduced now. The image for the plume on a helmet in Spenser (a slowly waving decorative detail) is appropriated by Tamburlaine. *He* is the 'almond tree ymounted high', and note how that archaic prefix for a past participle in Spenser—*y*mounting—gives the effect of a boost, of an aid to the 'mounting' in Marlowe. Not admiring the 'tree' from below, but rather being the tree, Tamburlaine naturally has to say the line quite otherwise than a reader of *The Faerie Queene* hears it said in Spenser's voice, and the word 'high' (following the spring, the lift from that prefix) rings out. But if Spenser is fairly collared here, the alexandrine ('At every little breath that thorow heauen is blowen') is less easily appropriated and tuned to a different note. The line is too long—the 'little' interferes in this meeting of pride, magnificence and energy—and the borrowed voice of Spenser and Marlowe's own voice together produce a kind of no-voice. But the genuine

[1] See Donald Davie: *Articulate Energy* (Routledge, 1955), for a full study of the effects of syntax on poetic results.

vaunting pitch is soon recovered, and more images of climbing, supremacy, dazzlement and joy are rung out.

This then is Marlowe's early voice which Alleyn was to relay with a harsh, wonderfully thrilled and thrilling, declamation. It had to be harsh and not shrill because of the bloody deeds necessary and intrinsic to the act of soaring. Moreover the violence and harshness of Marlowe's early voice follows on his being conscious that what he says is monstrously shocking and blasphemous. Of course Marlowe has to employ a surrogate for such shocking (that it is shocking is hugely relished) defiance, but it is Marlowe brandishing his wild banner all the same. Shelley, by contrast, could not be blasphemous if he tried, and he tried very hard but only to prove himself a universal philanthropist. This, though it shocked Oxford, won the genial approval of his 'idealistic' readers even if they were otherwise rather bored.

Marlowe-Tamburlaine defies; Shelley defies, notably in *Prometheus Unbound*, but the urge is then, as always in Shelley, masochistic: he is one of the beaten and bullied many who theoretically soars high to depose a tyrant; and, before that, rouses shrill notes of protest. Shelley is *in with* the victim, is not the tyrant or dictator. But, again, we are only considering a wish and an appropriate voice for the delivery of a wish. We must not put ourselves in the judgment seat and thereby, because of the voices they were born with, say which was the better poet. Both were superb, and we would be loth to lose either.

iii

We began by pointing a distinction between Marlowe and Shakespeare, but seem to have been sidetracked by pursuing distinctions between Marlowe and Spenser or Marlowe and Shelley. The main distinction between Marlowe and Shakespeare is between a poet who occupied the voices of his actors and a poet who was occupied by them. Here we remember the different educations of Shakespeare and Marlowe. It is not always lucky for a poet to go to Cambridge.

Now in *Tamburlaine* we find that the protagonist's disciples, Techelles and Usumcasane, and the rest of his supporters, simply speak as reflectors of the protagonist. 'Hear, hear', they call to each 'astounding term', to each asseveration of Tamburlaine's programme. Only their 'hear, hears' function as echoes: one or two notes higher in pitch than their leader's, harsh but less harsh than Tamburlaine's, because what they say is additive in intent and not original. Their voices are hoarse, metallic, energized by a will subscriptive to Tamburlaine's. Energized by will.

The difference of effect between Marlowe's imagery of mounting and soaring and Shelley's imagery of mounting and soaring is, in fact, produced by the kind of tense and Mood that each poet uses and to which his imagery is geared. As we have seen, the typical tense of Shelley in the mechanics of his poetry is the Future Conditional: 'O, that such and such *may* come about, and that the tyranny of kings and priests *may* end', sighingly exclaim his verbs. Then, in the operancy of his poetry (in the last Act of *Prometheus Unbound*, for instance), such and such does come about, the desired becomes actual and the voice lifts into a rapturous shrillness to which the volatile and dizzy imagery fits. It is otherwise with the verbs of Marlowe and, therefore, otherwise with his voice and otherwise with his spiritual temper, even though the imagery is similarly one of soaring and of icy peaks. Tamburlaine and his sycophantic chorus, Barabas and Faustus, each assert what they would do, or would have, or would know; would and so will (though they tragically fail). Each is an 'I' giving vent to his determination to glut a particular appetite.

This is something quite different from Shelley's generalized aspiration for human betterment, in which Shelley's 'I' becomes subsumed in the interest of the abstraction he calls 'Man', and points to another aspect of the famous speech ('Nature that fram'd us of foure Elements', etc.) of Tamburlaine deserving notice. The speech is unusual because the hero asserts that what drives him drives all others: we *all* thirst after the possession of an earthly crown. It seems here that Marlowe in being lyrical momentarily extricates himself from identity with the hero. Seeing his creature not so much separate from himself as parallel, Marlowe delivers himself of a manifesto which expresses the will of the two of them—to that extent the 'we' and the 'us' are justified—but which ought not to be understood as universal simply because of the occurrence of plural pronouns.

This is unusual because the identification of Marlowe with his protagonist is generally complete. But the absence of a dual form of the pronoun (an insulating form like *wit*—we two against the world) makes the speech seem illogical since, though one man may satisfy his urge to power by becoming a crowned tyrant, all men cannot. Multitudes of subjects will be needed, and if they are possessed of the same sustaining ambition they cannot be subjects for long.

But the important word is 'wils', and the significant tense of Marlowe, compelling the imagery of soaring and mounting, is the tense expressive of firm intention, the Future Indicative, governing an object which because of its infinite vastness is impossible to realize. '*I* will conquer the entire world and then the gods', '*I* will possess All-Knowledge and so absolute power', are the intentions of Tamburlaine and Faustus respectively. They do not satisfy their wills (whereas in Shelley the vastly aspired to becomes actual within the terms of the work), not because of the human opposition, which is feeble and dramatically unworthy, but because of the limitations imposed not so much by authoritarian gods (despite the conclusion of *Dr Faustus*) as by nature. But the tragic and sudden dénouements of both plays does not prevent the dominant voice of them being the voice of optimistic will. It is these daring assertions of will—what Tamburlaine, what Barabas, what Faustus, intend to *do* (with accompanying visual displays of interim token successes)—that makes the plays what they are. But the attitude of the hero is defiant, and because the spiritual state, not to say attitude, of defiance, calls for particular vocal tones, and because this defiance is quite brazen, the declaiming voice is, as it utters imagery of 'climbing', not like Shelley's but hard. It is unvarying in tempo, pitch and volume, as the hero proclaims his splendid mania. It is untinged by the tones of self-conscious nobility which colours Henry V's defiance at its most crassly savage, but this is because Henry, as a Christian, has always believed in human limitations.

This is to simplify for, as Marlowe proceeded on his brief career, his own voice—surviving his giant bullying protagonists—modulated gradually as the sheer subtlety of the opposition preventing full satisfaction came to be realized. All other human beings were inferior in *Tamburlaine* and could be sub-

dued, but nature overcame him in the end as he died from that
unromantic thing, mere illness or age. In *Dr Faustus* the
divine is also shown as hostile to the only worthy ambition. To
what extent does a progressive realization of the limits to human
will modify Marlowe's voice?

iv

The human checks to the magnificent bragging by Marlowe's
heroes of their accomplishments are dramatically weak. The
voices of Tamburlaine's antagonists are the voices of victims
and, since Marlowe is lending neither his sympathy nor his
voice to victims (but it he had lent, or given, his sympathy he
could not have withheld the voice), his victims are anonymous.
All the violence, all the 'fine madness' is vocalized by Tamburlaine, or the henchmen who add a line here or there which the
hero forgot. There is no pathos in the victims' lament, but there
is a caricature of pathos to raise laughs. To be pathetic is to be
weak and so hateful, and the voice for taunting weakness has
ever been jeering. Marlowe becomes a master of the jeering
voice—complementary on the passive side, the side of the victims, to the magnificent timbre, on the active side, of the heroes.
On the passive side: but this does not mean that he is identifying
himself with the victims, rather that he elicits from them the
whine the hero wants. It is a whine which arouses from the audience a laughter which the *victims* certainly do not mean to raise.
Yet it was this mode of response of the victims in a voice
collateral, so to speak, to the vaunting voice of the hero which
forced Marlowe to develop, having discovered it, aspects of his
own voice of which he had at first been unaware.

It has recently been suggested by Professor Clifford Leech[1]
that in *Edward II* Marlowe advances as a dramatist to the extent of distributing his sympathies: more, that in this play he is
identifying himself with the passive king rather than with the
active tyrant. Nevertheless, all critics have agreed that *Edward
II* reveals a decline in poetic power. No doubt it was difficult
for Marlowe to yield an original position so as to give sympathy
to suffering rather than to action. Apart from this, the work of

---

[1] In *The Critical Quarterly*, Vol. I, no. 4.

Marlowe reveals a gift radically different from Shakespeare's. In place of a poet who gradually abandoned, even lost, his own voice in the voices of others to become a dramatist, we have a poet who inflicted his own voice on a succession of heroes who turned the arena of their activity into one-man shows at the cost of suppressing countless personalities. But, at the end, in *Edward II*, Marlowe shows signs, not of losing his own voice to others, as did Shakespeare, but of transferring it to the weak opposition and giving to it the genuine expression of self-pity and despair.

PART FOUR

SOME RECENT VOICES AND CONCLUSION

IX *Some Recent Voices*

i

FOLLOWING our selective and recessional exploration in Parts Two and Three, the time has come to consider, though but very briefly, the voices of some of the poets of our own century. We begin with Hopkins, who is a poet of our century only because his voice was not effectually heard until forty-one years after his death in 1889.

As an unheard poet in the age of Tennyson's voice (for Tennyson had made his voice the voice of an age), Hopkins was aware of his difficulty in, literally, getting not a reading but a hearing. If anyone at all, outside his brethren in the Society of Jesus, should have known Hopkins' voice—so as to have been able to call it up in memory when confronted by something written in Hopkins' hand—then that someone was Bridges.[1] Bridges was a fine poet and a devoted friend, yet he would not (a failure of will) or could not (a failure of imaginative memory) hear the voice of Hopkins when he was sent the manuscript of *The Wreck of the Eurydice*. So Hopkins' reply is, in effect, 'please try to hear *me*': 'to do the Eurydice any kind of justice you must not slovenly read it with the eyes but with your ears, as if the paper were declaiming it at you . . . stress is the life of it.'[2]

Just so. But the voice Bridges *ought* to have heard the paper declaiming was that of Hopkins with the 'stress' peculiar to that voice. Bridges ought to have been able to have heard his absent friend's voice, to have imagined it, but yet he did not. On

---

[1] See *Robert Bridges and Gerard Hopkins 1863–1889. A Literary Friendship*, Jean-Georges Ritz (O.U.P., 1960).

[2] *The Letters of Gerard Manley Hopkins to Robert Bridges*, ed. C. C. Abbott, (O.U.P., 1935), pp. 51–52.

another occasion, Hopkins urged Bridges: 'Of this long sonnet, [*Spelt from Sibyl's Leaves*] above all remember what applies to all my verse, that it is, as living art should be, made for performance and that its performance is not reading with the eye but loud. This sonnet should be almost sung, it is most carefully timed in *tempo rubato*.'[1]

'Most carefully timed'—and Hopkins' accentual and expression marks help point the timing. Normally, the qualities of a voice, which are resistant to mensuration and notation, should declare themselves in a valid poem without attempting the inadequate aid of marks usually employed in the scoring of music, the whole context determining those qualities. But Hopkins was driven to add these aids in an effort to convey his own voice's mode of saying his poems—to convey it, if not to strangers, at least to friends and acquaintances. It is probable that Bridges, who in many respects had a keen and exquisite ear, did try to match what he saw to Hopkins' voice, as he remembered it, when *Eurydice* reached him through the post, but that the voice he remembered had altered; had necessarily altered as a consequence or concomitant of both the religious vocation (for we are bound to assume that conversion and vocation effected some sort of change in the structure of Hopkins' personality, and therefore of his voice) and of the 'new rhythm' which, after his long silence, had 'run through' Hopkins and compelled the making of *The Wreck of the Deutschland*.

If Bridges could only remember the voice of Hopkins the undergraduate, Dixon could only have remembered the voice of a schoolboy. Bridges and Dixon were alike sympathetic, but if they tried to affix the voice of someone they had once known to the poems of a Hopkins who had certainly changed, they were possibly in a worse position than complete strangers, just as an uncle or aunt who meets a nephew, after the lapse of one or two decades, understands the nephew less well than his recent acquaintance because he or she tries to see the new man as identical with the old child. The previous knowledge becomes not an aid but a hindrance to understanding.

[1] P. 246, *op. cit.* Elsewhere he writes: 'My verse is less to be read than heard, as I have told you before; it is oratorical, that is the rhythm is so. I think if you will study what I have here said you will be much more pleased with it and may I say? converted to it.' *Ibid.*, p. 46.

Further: if Bridges' and Dixon's experience of Hopkins' voice
had been confined to hearing that voice in conversation, they
have this excuse—that a voice is transformed, or releases un-
suspected qualities, when it is lifted or controlled by poetic
rhythm. We noticed that Shelley's unpleasant speaking voice
became 'good both in tune and tone' when he read verse[1]—
the rhythm resolving the discordances. Any kind of rhythm
would have exerted some influence on Hopkins' normal speaking voice, but the 'new rhythm', to which he referred, would
have keyed it up and released what was essentially unique about
it, its 'instress'.

Coventry Patmore was not at this disadvantage of previous
acquaintance. He encountered the poems in manuscript before
he met the man at all, for Bridges had sent them to him without
Hopkins' permission. And Patmore wrote to their author: 'My
difficulty in getting at anything very new is as I said before,
greater than of most persons and sometimes that difficulty
seems insuperable. It struck me, however, at once, in reading
your poems, that the key to them might be supplied by your
own reading of them, and I trust some day to have the benefit
of that assistance.'[2]

There is no evidence that Patmore ever enjoyed that assistance, and perhaps no one ever heard Hopkins reading his poetry
aloud during his lifetime.

It was only during the early 1930's that some came to hear
his voice with the inner ear. In the process of reconstruction
of a dead man's voice, it was found that the 'stress-marks' and
'marks of expression' were dispensable. They suggested, rather
than defined, a particular vocal movement. But once the movement was perceived (or heard) it became clear that only a
peculiar timbre—a timbre expressive of a keyed-upness, an
intensity—would go with that movement. Remembering not
only the keyed-upness of *The Windhover* or *God's Grandeur*, but

---

[1] See p. 69 above.

[2] Further *Letters of Gerard Manley Hopkins*, ed. C. C. Abbot (O.U.P., 1956),
Letter CLXXVI E, p. 354. Patmore is strikingly honest in confessing his
difficulty. What is essential, in his confession, is the 'very new'. Patmore
could have recognized a familiar voice, or the voice of someone imitating a
familiar voice, but he could not place or invent a voice appropriate to
Hopkins' verses. Patmore himself, among the Victorians, had a strikingly
individual voice.

the exaltation with which they begin, and end by surpassing, it is not surprising that it is reported of his voice that 'it tended to be shrill'.[1] The timbre and tendency to shrillness once heard, then the right play and positioning of 'stress', and the degree and kind of 'expression' to be infused, became apparent. Yet that timbre, though it has now been heard in the auditory imagination of many, resists definition. It can be precisely heard in the auditory imagination but resists precise definition. But we can point to the fact that the affirmations of *God's Grandeur*, and the facts stated in *The Windhover* alike require clusters of verbs in the Indicative Mood and simple straightforward constructions. The poems possess these grammatical and syntactical features (for the piling up of adjectives and the omission of articles do not destroy the simplicity of construction), and they become instruments tuned to the keen voice of exaltation.

Hopkins' voice had its *haecceitas*, and it cannot be denied that the publication of the Correspondence and the Note-books have assisted us in realizing it. In these, it is true, Hopkins was observing, contemplating, praying, pleading or persuading in prose. But in the act of observing, contemplating, praying, pleading and persuading he became aware of the 'selfness' of his essential voice. It may even be easier for some to hear Hopkins in his poetry by way of first hearing him in prose.

ii

We turn next to some poets who have an advantage over their predecessors: their voices have been mechanically recorded. Broadcasts or records of Yeats, Eliot, Auden and others, saying their own poems can, and should be, adduced as a test of what we have said of other poets who lived and died before the gramophone was invented. Perhaps we were too hasty with that 'advantage'. Though this is an age of broadcasting, tape recorders, amplifiers and record players we cannot say that the poet's condition has yet very much changed in consequence. It may never. All we can say is that the poet's relation with his public has potentially altered: that in the future he might return

[1] See Christopher Devlin, S.J.: *The Sermons and Devotional Writings of Gerard Manley Hopkins* (O.U.P., 1959), p. 5.

to finding himself primarily addressing listeners in the plural
rather than a reader in the singular. Might return: the point
has not yet been reached when poets largely compose for live
or mechanical sound transmission, and it is mentioned now
simply to bring into realization the fact that Yeats, Eliot and
Auden are, by an accident of time, recorded saying their
poems aloud whereas earlier poets were not.

W. B. Yeats is one of the few English poets who composed,
with no major break, throughout a long life. After a certain age
he did not simply draw on the reserves of memory (as Wordsworth was well-nigh forced to do) but, on the contrary, changed
his style (as they say) as his being changed. He began, as a poet,
in the misty mournful twilight of the Celtic fringe and ended
among the cold hard clarity of the Byzantine mosaics. He began with *The Lake Isle of Innisfree* and *The Countess Cathleen* and he
ended—by way of *Easter 1916*—with

> This is no country for old men. The young
> In one another's arms . . .

What is here proposed is that no such series of stylistic changes
could have been rendered, had not vocal changes kept even
pace. For Yeats, throughout this series of changes, composed
with a vivid awareness of what he was writing being actually
heard. Everywhere, as V. C. Clinton-Baddeley avers, he insisted on the line being taken as a line; the line was a rhythmical
unit and had to be marked by a pause at its conclusion.[1]

Throughout he was voicing himself. *The Lake Isle of Innisfree*
was not recorded within decades of its composition, if at all, but
we must presume, if sound and sense are allowed a correlation,
that it was imagined as being said in a soft but lilting, a vague
yet determinedly nostalgic (and thoroughly Irish) voice,
whereas in *Easter 1916* the voice is roused to a tense and hard—
and passionate—intensity. Come down further in time, and those

[1] See V. C. Clinton-Baddeley: 'Reading Poetry with W. B. Yeats'
(*London Magazine*, vol. 4, no. 12, pp. 47–53). Baddeley was rehearsing at the
BBC the lines quoted above and found difficulty in giving a syntactical
pause after 'men' *and* after 'young'. Yeats, in the control room, noting the
hesitation, said 'Worse piece of syntax I ever wrote' and pencilled a line in
his copy (which has not been accepted by later editions) 'Old men should
quit this country where the young . . .'

who heard Yeats broadcast his later poems in the thirties will recall the quavering impassioned chaunting of his delivery of the Byzantine poems. They will also remember his vocal realization of the poems with a refrain, the care and force with which he distinguished the refrains (dry and high-pitched) from the stanzas to which they subscribed. If, previous to Yeats' own rendering, some of us had failed, depending on the printed signs alone, to hear him, then we can admit that memories of his broadcasts have enabled us to apply the memory of his voice to the printed signs so that they are no longer mute. But so much can be admitted of recordings made by other poets: if we had not previously heard their voices behind and through the printed pages—if we had lacked the vocal imagination, that is, to construct their voices—then we can now apply our memory of the actual living voice to poems that otherwise would not have spoken to us; and when once poems have spoken to us they are accepted as part of our experience.[1] But, since a poet's voice changes, it is desirable indeed that he should record his poems (I refer to those poems which are worth recording) before they are distant to himself in time, removed from his own sympathy, and have lapsed to a dead era of his voice which he can no longer reproduce.

iii

The Love Song of J. Alfred Prufrock, composed 1910–11,[2] was not recorded by Mr Eliot until much later. No doubt this recording still possesses a kind of interest and a kind of authority not possessed by other people's performances of the same poem: even so the interest consists partly in the realization that here a poet is having to remember and—in remembering—act a voice and personality that lay a quarter of a century in the past. It might even be thought he is having to remember two voices and

---

[1] Those who heard Dylan Thomas declaiming his poems on the radio, or who have heard the gramophone recordings, might ask themselves whether they think Thomas would have composed the kind of poetry that he did but for the possession of a vocal instrument so exactly suitable for its rendering.

[2] See Hugh Kenner: *The Invisible Poet* (W. H. Allen, 1960), pp. 3–11.

two personalities—his own and his persona's, Mr Prufrock's,[1]
and, that in remembering them, he has to forget all that has
since superintervened. By contrast, the gramophone recordings
of *The Four Quartets* were made soon after the poems' publication.
Moreover, besides being made when they were still fresh and
close to him in time, The Quartets, unlike the dramatic mono-
logues of the pre-*Ash Wednesday* period, are clearly 'I' poems—
poems conceived as being spoken in the author's voice.

We must suppose that the slow growth of Mr Eliot's fame can be
largely explained by the sheer difficulty of the earliest reviewers
in attaching any sort of convincing voice to the words on the page.
The words as such—when read merely with the eye and mind, as
most prose is intended to be read—were not difficult. The difficulty lay in fitting a voice to the words so that they became, beyond their prose meaning, poetic in depth. Failing to construct in
the aural imagination the author's voice, with its peculiar timbre,
the first reviewers in 1917, confronted with *Prufrock and Other
Observations*, either heard nothing at all, and simply regarded the
purely semantic content of the lines, or they tried to fit the signs on
the page to the voices of other poets whom they did know, or to
their own voices. But the pages before them were resistant to the
application of any other voice outside the author's, resistant to
other individual voices and resistant to the collective voice of the
Georgians—for such normative or collective voices certainly
exist. This predicament explains the review of the book in *The
Times Literary Supplement*: 'Mr Eliot's notion of poetry—he calls
the "observations" poems—seems to be a purely analytical treatment, varying sometimes in the catalogue, of personal relations
and environment, uninspired by any glimpse beyond them and
untouched by any genuine rush of feeling. As even, on this basis,
he remains frequently inarticulate, his "poems" will hardly be
read by many with enjoyment.'[2]

[1] 'Two voices.' But, whatever the stimulus provided by Laforgue, Eliot in
a thoroughly Browningesque manner would seem able to assert in his own
voice, through the protective mask of Mr Prufrock, that which explicit self-
expression would have been incapable of asserting. *Prufrock* is not dramatic
in the sense that *La Jeune Parque* is dramatic—a poem which, Valéry said,
could only be recited by a contralto voice. See Francis Scarfe, 'A Note on
the Monologue', pp. 107–136, in *The Art of Paul Valéry* (Heinemann, 1956).

[2] Reprinted in a special issue of *The Times Literary Supplement*, 18 January,
1952, p. 56.

The reviewer could not hear an original voice (one encounters everywhere, so that it has become a critical cliché, the phrase 'the poet's voice', but here the phrase is meant to be taken literally), so what he saw with his eye, and noted with his mind, were—and so they remained—a series of signs indicating a number of 'observations'. The transaction between writer and reviewer was solely mental and silent. But this is not to deny that this reviewer may not have had an acute and subtle ear for voices of poets which had established themselves, and of which he had taken possession, for, say, Wordsworth's (yet *The Times Literary Supplement* review reminds one of an early review of *The Lyrical Ballads*, which is less surprising when one remembers that the first reviewers of *The Lyrical Ballads* were trying to fasten what they read to the voice of Pope or to the voices of those much later who echoed—at a remote distance—the voice of Pope), or Tennyson's, or for those sub-Tennysonian voices among the Georgians. He probably, indeed, had a keen ear for many sub-Tennysonian voices, and could have distinguished one from another within the genus— (Brooke's from Flecker's, say, both interesting voices, and the degree to which the latter's personal voice is overlaid by Swinburne's and by certain French poets', in addition to Tennyson's—which he was fighting against—adds to their contrast), but not for a St Louis-Boston voice somewhat disguised by attempts to catch the accents, or vocal individuality, of Europe —of Paris more than London.

That reviewer did not hear, but since 1917 Mr Eliot has made it clear that his voice and the printed lines of his verse do indeed match; match so that it is difficult to avoid hearing that voice now, even when it is distributed among characters in one of the later plays—so difficult that readers may sometimes doubt whether the characters have voices of their own at all.

Since 1917 Mr Eliot's poetry—and therefore his voice—has gradually altered, but his listeners, having possessed themselves of the earlier stages, can now accept each new stage as a natural extension in the order of development, and hence they recognize that a recorded speaking of *J. Alfred Prufrock* made in 1936 is a different and less urgent thing than the one that was *not* made in 1917. Born one year before Hopkins died, Mr Eliot succeeded in transmitting his voice some eight years before

Hopkins transmitted his. Now, in 1962, both voices are heard well enough. But whether those born during, or after the second world war, who are inclined to make their first acquaintance of Eliot through his plays will be able, as they follow his history from the reverse direction, to possess the earliest voice is an interesting question. For the slump in the prestige of Tennyson, and of other poets, a decade or so after their deaths is perhaps to be attributed to a new generation, made familiar by their parents with the dead poet's most mature—or latest—works, but ignorant of the earliest, resisting the voice of an elderly man only because they had not begun at the other end and followed the history of that voice from the time it was as young as their own.

iv

No one, if technology had been advanced enough, would have recorded Keats, but Byron would certainly have been recorded (and televised) soon after the publication of *Childe Harold* I and II. Let us conclude this section on the voice of a living poet who made, like Byron, an immediate impact, albeit on a diminished scale. W. H. Auden was early recorded, as Byron would have been recorded; and Auden has been much indebted to—or influenced by—Byron.

W. H. Auden is a poet who has been recorded saying his own verse, at frequent and fairly regular intervals, since he first became prominent. These records are the best of documents and the documents are available. We are enabled to appraise and to study the development of Auden in the light of these documents,[1] to an extent that is hardly possible in the cases of other, and more considerable, poets. This is because whereas Eliot was not recorded, as far as I am aware, saying his early poems before 1936, when those poems lay distant in his past, removed by time from his active sympathy and not adjusted to their still proprietorial voice because it had changed, Auden was recorded saying his earliest poems when they were still fresh to him. And since then each new volume of verse has been closely followed by excerpts recorded in his own voice.

[1] '*In the light of* these documents.' The visual metaphor belongs to an age of mute documents. The solecism reminds us of the difficulties that dying habits impose.

Consequently we have here an instance of a poet with a long career—some thirty years at the moment of writing—of almost continuous production, which production has been almost simultaneously preserved in two media. In two media: yet, if we are at all correct, the one medium (print) is in fact only a substitute, or a series of signs for, the other—the other being supplied, in default of the living voice of the poet, by the 'reader', or listener, who may have to regard the printed signs as a code to be cracked. In Auden's case this parallel preservation has this value: we can relate what is customarily called 'stylistic development' to changes in the poet's physical voice as revealed by the recordings. Now in 1936 Auden recorded 'A Bride in the 30's', beginning:

> Easily, my dear, you move, easily your head,
> And easily as through leaves of a photograph album I'm led
> Through the night's delights and the day's impressions,
> Past the tall tenements and the trees in the wood,
> Though sombre the sixteen skies of Europe
>   And the Danube flood.
>
> Looking and loving our behaviours pass
> The stones, the steels, and the polished glass;
> Lucky to Love the new pansy railway,
> The sterile farms where his looks are fed,
> And in the policed unlucky city
>   Lucky his bed.
>
> He from these lands of terrifying mottoes
> Makes worlds as innocent as Beatrix Potter's;
> Through breakfast countries where they mend the roads
> Along the endless plains his will is,
> Intent as a collector, to pursue
>   His greens and lilies . . .[1]

and in 1954 he recorded the following passage from *The Sea and the Mirror*, 'Alonso to Ferdinand':

> Dear son, when the warm multitudes cry,
> Ascend your throne majestically,
> But keep in mind the waters where fish
> See sceptres descending with no wish
> To touch them; sit regal and erect,

[1] BBC Record no. 2160, library no. 1497c, recorded January 27, 1936.

186

But imagine the sands where a crown
Has the status of a broken-down
Sofa or multilated statue:
Remember as bells and cannon boom
The cold depth that does not envy you
The sunburnt superficial kingdom
Where a king is an object.

Expect no help from others, for who
Talk sense to princes or refer to
The scorpion in official speeches
As they unveil some granite Progress
Leading a child or holding a bunch
Of lilies? In their Royal Zoos the
Shark and the octopus are tactfully
Omitted: synchronized clocks march on
Within their powers: without, remain
The ocean flats where no subscription
Concerts are given, the desert plain
Where there is nothing for lunch . . .[1]

What is the relation, in each case, between the voice speaking
the poem and the corresponding text? The voice in the 1954
recording can certainly be identified as the voice of eighteen
years earlier, but, just as certainly, the voice has undergone
changes. Since 1936 it has dropped and settled at a lower pitch.
It has become to a slight, but appreciable degree, American-
ized. Since the creation of speech sounds, according to special
modes of organization, is the peculiar activity of the poet, this
Americanization means, on the evidence of this changed
physical utterance of English, that the poet Auden has changed.
In the 'A Bride in the 30's', the voice exploited variations of
pitch and tone. In 'Alonso to Ferdinand' the voice—while preserving its earlier characteristic metallic timbre—proceeds at a
constant pitch, tone and pace. More generally, the voice of 'A
Bride in the 30's' is lighter, is that of a sophisticated young
upper-middle class Oxford graduate, a master of the 'airy
manner' and almost too dreadfully knowing. Since then, over

[1] Library of Congress, Washington, D.C., P.L.I. Since *The Sea and the
Mirror* was published in 1945, the recording was not made hard after
composition. But it was made near enough to support the argument.

the years, it has become gradually deeper and graver, and yet less flexible. The process continues. If the voice behind *The Sea and the Mirror* is the voice of the mandarin, the voice behind *Nones* is the voice of the preacher. Thus the development of Auden's style on the printed page, from *Look, Stranger!* onwards, corresponds with the development of his physical voice. It also shows that subsequent alterations that Auden makes to his early poems, separated from his present being by a quarter of a century or more, can do harm besides the injury of altering their intention in order that they comport with his later Christian outlook. However critical of the younger man the older man may be, the judicial act of altering what he once wrote amounts to a denial of their original validity (their local and temporal validity at the time of first composition) and of his earlier personality and of the voice adjusted to that personality. The interpolations of passages in one voice, that were originally cast and spoken in another, a process quite different from that which can fairly be called revision,[1] results in a poem that belongs to *no* voice, that cannot be spoken aloud because the vocal text of the original is nonplussed by incursions in another tone which denies the existence of the first.

Auden perhaps scarcely approaches the greatness of the other poets we have considered. Nevertheless the existing series of records that keeps step with the phases of his career affords evidence for the proposition that poets write the history of their voices.

[1] For the intention of revision is not only to improve, it is also to make inharmonious parts consonant with the work as a whole. Revision aims not at changing the intention of a work, but at altering recalcitrant parts so that they conform with that intention.

X Conclusion

i

IN Part Two we attempted to bring into awareness three individual physical voices which we ought to hear behind—or through—the printed 'Poetical Works' of Tennyson, Shelley and Milton. Assuredly those physical voices existed and assuredly the printed signs on the page are *not* the poems. We have suggested that each of these poets conceived and 'wrote' in terms of his own voice—not, probably, as it actually was, as it actually sounded to others, that is, but as the poet himself heard it, or experienced it, or (such qualifications are necessary because so little is known about the whole matter) as he supposed it to sound to others when he was employing it to good effect. Yet however we interpret the phrase 'his own voice', and however much or little we suppose each poet was conscious of an audience, this conclusion has been reached: that the work of these three poets was to some extent controlled, to some extent limited therefore, by the properties of their actual physical voices. Beside these three 'I' poets (the homophone 'eye' is unfortunate: the genuine eye-poet is a mathematician), we have set, in Part Three, Shakespeare, a poet who, though he 'wrote' the *Sonnets* in terms of his own voice, ended by 'writing' for the actual voices of others—or for imagined or remembered voices which the known actual voices could render—and for which he composed more abundantly, more successfully, and of course with a far greater range of effects, though 'effects' is here a cheap word.

Yet a question which might have been irking the minds of readers is this: If we have not been treated to a confusion between the voice of the poetry (where 'voice' is not literal but has reference to an imagined voice of the poet imaginatively apprehended and heard by the reader with the ear of imagination—that 'inner ear'), has not this enquiry simply resolved itself into an analysis of the styles of different writers?

The answer is, I believe, not at all. *Le style est l'homme* perhaps, but only inasmuch as the man has elected one manner of speaking or writing more than another, or inasmuch as he has trained his real voice or the voice which seems to be real to himself.

Style can refer as much to spoken as to written language. Now there is certainly a linguistic property, many would call a 'style', possessed by the dialogue of a play by Congreve or Oscar Wilde. This 'style' reflects the tone, temper or—again—'style' of actual conversation of particular castes of society in the days of Congreve and in the days of Wilde. But, depending on the degree to which Congreve and Wilde succeeded in their aims, I would prefer to consider their 'styles' echoes—echoes perfected, formalized, patterned—of a caste or collective voice, and to urge that, in the case of the 'I' poets, so far contemplated, we have been less occupied by an attempt to define a period or caste mode of speaking, than to explore precious—precious, because strictly unique—individualities. A period or caste mode of speaking may, through its system of accented predilections, modify the individual timbre of a voice so as to muffle it into unimportance. Perhaps Shelley had, in a sense, an upper class Regency voice and Tennyson a barely upper-middle class Victorian one—barely because of the Lincolnshire 'accent'. But that is not the point of our present enquiry of these 'I' poets: the point being instead a discussion of our auditory response to a quality existing below a style as imposed by the discipline of a caste or period, a quality—namely timbre—almost or entirely suppressed by a social comedy imitative of manners, but present, and of primary importance, in lyric poetry and in other kinds of poetry where the poet is speaking in his own person.

Further, the word 'style' more particularly connotes things admirable to the sight—a written or printed page or a décor—connotations we have been especially anxious to avoid. A 'style' is taught or adopted. A person may be trained in, or he may adopt, a manner—or 'style' (for that is what a 'style' is, a manner)—of writing, or speaking or of deportment, or of dress, or of anything else. In the process of training a man might alter the management of his voice so that it might seem other than it is—might seem representative of a group or 'set' rather than continue to be an index or betrayal of personality. But a voice's timbre *underlies* 'style'. A person's voice is something he inherits, but which environment modifies and on which experience tells. In creating sound waves it reveals its owner's personality, or, in sounding 'through the mask', it betrays the reality behind the 'personality'. It will vary according to age or mood; it may be shaped or patterned by imitation or training so that in its employment it partakes of a 'style'; but it is a man's own—not any other man's—and so unique.

Why have I selected the poets that I have and not others? Because, in the cases of Tennyson and Shelley the evidence exists as to their very different kinds of voices and some evidence also, especially in the case of Tennyson, as to their ways of using their voices when they said their poems aloud. That this evidence corroborates what we might have guessed on the testimony of our own experience—namely: of what we hear with the inner ear when we read their poetry—is exactly to our purpose. I selected Milton, not only because of the scraps of evidence which exist as to the kind of voice he had, but also because the blind author of *Paradise Lost* was eminently preoccupied by sound; and he dictated his poem. There is also the testimony of his spelling and punctuation. Also, it was perhaps obviously clearer of Milton than of many poets that his maturing (and so altering) voice was the foundation of his 'style', that the 'stylistic' difference between *l'Allegro* and *Paradise Lost* must suppose a change in physical voice.[1]

That I have, as it turns out, chosen for particular study just the three 'I' poets who, during the thirties, endured those critical revaluations which severely damaged their reputations,

---

[1] For what it is worth, here is the result of a brief and not very thorough experiment: The consultation of a number of Concordances to the major poets, under such headings as 'voice' and 'sound' (singly or as elements of compound words) revealed that Tennyson, Shelley and Milton were consistently more concerned with voices and with sound—judging merely by the frequencies of these words in their works—than other poets, with the probable exception of Wordsworth.

is accidental. But those revaluations may have been unconsciously motivated by an animus against three voices precisely because they were so unmistakeably clear and individual—so clear that they resisted, more intransigently than other voices, all attempts to include or smother them in the critics' own voices, or the period voice of the thirties? Or, perhaps, because Tennyson, Shelley and Milton had, in their several ways, such splendid—in addition to being so distinctly individual, splendid—voices, some of their critics' inability to imitate or echo them accurately and effectively, when they tried to quote them aloud, produced in these critics a dislike of the voices? Rather than own their antipathy to these physical voices, or confess their failure to echo them, or, even, their inability or refusal to hear them, is it not possible that these critics said, 'Listen, how pretentious and absurd these poets sound!'—and then read them aloud (or heard them) not in the poets', or in a fair imitation of the poets', but in their own voices? In that case, they—both the poets and the critics—would indeed have sounded pretentious and absurd.

Of Shakespeare's voice we have no external documentary evidence. But there is the evidence of his work. And his work included the *Sonnets* and these are 'I' poems. We have applied what we have learned of later 'I' poets to the Shakespeare of the *Sonnets* and then compared the result with, first the singular voice, and then the plural voices of the plays. But this has been, confessedly, a speculative effort. Shakespeare, alone of the poets of whom we have treated at length, was not almost wholly possessed by his own voice: instead, on the contrary, he came to possess—so as to use—the voices of others. Through using the throats of others as his instruments he came in time to command many voices. By habitually employing these instruments they became in time less extensions of Shakespeare than part of him. He gradually became multi-voiced. But anything like a full exploration of the implications of this last statement—or, if the statement is accepted, of the histories of these voices and their inter-relationships—must lie outside the scope of our present enquiry.

Apart from the recognition that English is changing, and that it is easier to approach Milton by way of the intermediaries between him and us than through his predecessors (or that it is easier to approach Chaucer by way of Shakespeare than through Mannyng), and that we can catch Tennyson's voice sooner, simply because its sound waves have barely ceased reverberating, there was a reason for treating the voices of Tennyson, Shelley, Milton and Shakespeare in the reverse of their order in time. The descriptions of Tennyson's voice are more numerous than the descriptions of Shelley's; those of Shelley closer and more extensive than those of Milton's. Of Shakespeare's voice no accounts have survived, and there we must rely entirely on the poetry he wrote for his own and other voices. But though the external evidence decreases as we go back in time we need not therefore feel proportionately more confident that we know Tennyson's voice better than the others. If the wealth of evidence here encourages us to exclaim, 'What his contemporaries said about Tennyson's voice agrees with what we had previously imagined', then that gives us some encouragement for relying rather more than otherwise we would have done on the voices we had imagined for other poets where there is no external evidence. If it simply corroborates what we had previously heard when 'reading' Tennyson's poetry, then the poetry itself, and not the contemporary descriptions, is clearly our chief source of information. This is as much as to say that if we want to know what a man's voice is like—what, therefore, *he* is like— we would do better to hear the man himself speaking rather than read descriptions of his voice by others. Through the totality of the printed signs on the page the poet conveys his voice.[1] To respond to this totality—the sense is included as well

[1] Some linguists might protest that even if a writer [*sic*] had used the phonetic alphabet of the *Association Phonétique Internationale*, in place of English conventional spelling, that still much of the individuality of his voice would be lost; not merely his phonemes, but the parameters of speech generally. To this I would reply that the word 'writer' will not do for a 'poet' and especially not for an 'I' poet; and that a poet conveys his voice to the listener not with, but through and despite of, typography, and that the semantics (by which I here include feeling as well as meaning) of his lines and phrases govern the recreation of his voice in the reader's imagination no less than does the phonology. Of course it is realized that poets such as Shakespeare and Milton have the advantage over Shelley and Tennyson in this respect: the two former, in their use of orthographics and punctuations more personal, had notational systems more eloquent of themselves. To this extent the voice of a seventeenth-century poet is better recorded than the voice of a nineteenth-century poet.

as the sound, since they are as inseparable as mind and body, the one is what it is because of the other—is an act of the auditory imagination.

I believe that such acts of auditory imagination or empathy are primary for the reception and so enjoyment of poetry, and that the discovery of how they may be accomplished is more valuable to a student than a too early acquisition of the 'know-how' of practical criticism. This acquisition is always too early if it results in the exercise of adjudicative power on 'specimens' which are only *seen* on the page before being submitted to the procrustean bed of a taught method. Proud is the adjudicative power if it exists alone, and destructive too if it is given a 'know-how'; if this power exists with others then it can behave admirably so long as it supports rather than precedes them.

ii

What would we not give for a gramophone record of Wordsworth reading his poems aloud during the period covered by Dorothy's journal? or of Keats saying his Odes? or of Hopkins declaiming *The Wreck of the Deutschland*?

Yet those who know their Wordsworth, or their Keats, or their Hopkins, know them as voices as well as others know Shelley's voice in the light of the pages of T. J. Hogg. Irritatingly patronizing as it often is, that attributive form, 'If you know your . . .', has this in its favour: when one says that someone knows 'his' Wordsworth one is saying someone *possesses* Wordsworth. That is scarcely metaphorical. Habitual reading of a poet enables the reader to possess, as it were, that poet's voice so that he recognizes a chance quotation from the poet, and he signals his recognition by saying, 'I don't know where it comes from but it sounds like ——', naming the poet. 'Sounds like': it is not the rhythm or the imagery or the themes that endow a poet with his unique sound. These, and other factors, modify the sound but all are finally symptomatic of the voice. The last stage of acquaintance with a poet occurs when one can hear the voice in absence of the text or, in presence of the text, when the signs on the page no longer act as intermediary but instantaneously conduct.

Since the evidence for the voices of most dead poets exists not

externally but in the imaginations of those who hear them—
though those imaginations are controlled by the printed signs
standing for this or that man's 'poetical works'—it will be said
that such evidence, though abundant, is subjective. It is subjective because it depends on all those who know 'their' Browning, or 'their' Keats, or 'their' Wordsworth, or 'their' Gray, etc.,
agreeing as to what they hear when they hear the voice of
those poets. How to test the measure of their agreement?

Those who know, say, their *Elegy in the Churchyard* will (within
narrow limits) agree as to whether a recital of the poem is good
or bad. It will be good or bad according to how near the voice
of the reciter approaches, or falls short of, the agreed known
voice of Gray *in this particular poem*. It might be objected that
this is dangerous because there is no gramophone record of
Gray to corroborate the impression of his voice in the inner
hearing of those who 'possess' the poem: that all we have urged
is unprovable. Some might declare that if a reliable gramophone record of Gray saying the poem *were* discovered, those
who know 'their' Gray would be disconcerted—literally—by
the actual voice. But not only is that equally unprovable, but it
would suggest that Gray was either being a poetic dramatist in
his *Elegy*—an absurd position—or that there was a wide dis-
crepancy between Gray's actual voice and his ideal voice.

Moreover, one would reply that the eighteenth century was
still a period when poetry was mainly a said and heard thing;
that we are long before the theory of a Yeatsian mask or a
Poundian persona; also, that the voice of the *Elegy*, though requiring a smaller volume of voice than that required for a
ceremonial Ode such as *The Bard* (the imagined acoustics for
the reception of this poem were different), shows a consistency
with the rest of the work summarized under the title of 'Gray's
Poetical Works'. One would also reply, that did the external evidence exist, as it does exist in the case of Tennyson or of Shelley,
that it would substantiate the position of those who know
'their' Gray, who feel that only one voice can be fitted to these
lines:

> Can storied urn or animated bust
> Back to its mansion call the fleeting breath?
> Can Honour's voice provoke the silent dust?
> Or Flatt'ry soothe the dull cold ear of Death?

and that that voice is the poet's: for not only do the lines bespeak a particular mood governing a particular tone and tempo,
not only does the distribution of vowels require a particular
tonic pitch, but these—plus other indicators, semantic, phono-
logical, physical—contribute towards, and compel, a timbre
and a series of vocal harmonics, that only one voice could
produce. That voice is Gray's. We heard it with our inner ear
at the moment we first possessed the poem: Gray had then said it
aloud to us.

Once Gray has said it aloud to us in this sense we will have
experienced an ideal reading. For however we modulate our
own voices to correspond with what we hear, or have heard,
the correspondence will never be exact, since our voices are no
less severally unique than was Gray's. That is true, and the best
we can hope for, when the poem is said aloud, is a voice which
approaches Gray's as nearly as possible. A voice which is naturally close to Gray's will have the advantage. If the voice, which
attempts the poem, is naturally remote from Gray's then, whatever modulations the reader affects, in striving to imitate what
he has heard, the audience will be dissatisfied. The audience
will be still more dissatisfied if it becomes apparent from the
reading that the performer has never even heard Gray's voice.

These are severe remarks, but let us remember that the voices
of poets differ so widely that none of us, however accurately we
hear them, can ever hope to reproduce all of them, however
flexible or sympathetic one's own voice may be. We must also
remember that none of us has an inner ear so catholic that it has
even heard the whole variety of voices, English and foreign.
Most of us are deaf to at least one other poet speaking to us
from the past, and deaf to several speaking to us in the present.
But we can at least hope that this or that voice, to which we are
deaf, may perhaps suddenly break through to us in the future—
to our personal gain, a gain because enlargement. We can
reasonably hope for this on the ground of experience. For
surely it has happened to many of us that a poet, to whom we
had been deaf, has suddenly spoken to us. We had read with
the eye the pages of this poet's work and been unmoved. Then,
unexpectedly, we have heard this poet speaking to us in one
poem, and now, having heard his voice in that one poem, we
can turn back to the work, which we had previously only seen,

and we can apply that voice. This is not to say that the new voice which we now possess, or inhabit, would not vary from one kind of poem to another kind of poem, from one decade of his life to another; for we have demonstrated that a poet's voice—though an identity—does indeed vary according to his mood, his age, the kind and size of audience he is actually or supposedly addressing, the acoustics he imagines.

Index

INDEX

INDEX